The Irrepressible David F. Day

By Duane A. Smith

WESTERN REFLECTIONS PUBLISHING COMPANY®

Lake City, CO

ISBN 978-1-932738-85-8

Library of Congress Control Number: 2010921520

Cover photo: Western Historical Collection, University
of Colorado
Cover and text design: Laurie Goralka Design

First Edition
Printed in the United States of America

Western Reflections Publishing Company®
P.O. Box 1149
951 N. Highway 149
Lake City, CO 81235
www.westernreflectionspublishing.com

For my friend, James Sheppard,
Who claims he waited "decades for my book."

TABLE OF CONTENTS

INTRODUCTION

Having run across David Frakes Day during many research projects, I became fascinated by the man and his writings. Popular and controversial in his day, his newspaper represented 19th century Colorado journalism at its best, although some of his contemporaries might take umbrage at such a statement. Day would not have minded; he loved a good controversy, a good fight. The more the better. These scrapes helped popularize and sell his *Solid Muldoon*.

For a little more than a decade, he lived in Ouray, a beautiful mountain setting but an isolated community, until the Denver & Rio Grande Railroad finally arrived in 1887. In the years that followed, the town prospered as a mining center, tourist mecca, and, with its hot springs, a health spa. Its outspoken, quotable editor also did his share to keep the community in the public's eye.

As might be imagined, his outspokenness stirred strong feelings and animosities. Add to these some local land speculation that might have undermined Ouray's getting the much needed railroad connection, and Day became a *persona non-grata* to many of the townspeople.

According to local lore, Durango Democrats, upset because their town's newspapers were Republican oriented, invited Day to move to their community. For whatever reason, a group of men definitely invited Day to come. He moved south from Ouray in March, 1892. One of these men, driven to the point of exasperation by the ornery Day, complained later that he put up $800 to "get the old man over here," and now he was "damned if he wouldn't give twice that amount to send him back." Meanwhile, his *Solid Muldoon* name was dropped, and Day continued on with the *Durango Democrat*.

Day would remain in Durango the rest of his life, dying there on June 22, 1914. Looking back from 1942, his son George Vest Day summarized his dad's newspaper career as well as anyone. "Father's idea of a good time was a scrap for what he thought was right, the bigger the better."

Day's long-time rival, the *Durango Herald* (June 22), paid tribute to him. "His passing takes away one of the best known pioneers of the state as well as one of its ablest newspapermen. As a paragrapher he was conceded to be without equal and his clever caustic pen brought him national recognition."

The *Democrat* offered further tribute to its founder and long time editor.

> *Col. Day, in his public life, has always been known and respected as a fearless fighter for the right. He has, by reason of his wonderful prescience, been able to forecast correctly events in public matters during all his public life. . . . He made many enemies by his fearless and outspoken manner, but these are vastly outnumbered by the friends he has made, and even his enemies respected him for his integrity.*
>
> *In the loss of Col. Day the city of Durango, the San Juan Basin and the state of Colorado loses a valuable citizen.*

The hope of this book is to bring David Day, his times and his newspaper to life again for twenty-first century readers. To do this, the years from September 5, 1879, through March 7, 1885, of the weekly *Solid Muldoon* were chosen, along with a few issues of the daily *Muldoon*, published only briefly in October and November of 1882, as a political sheet during a heated campaign.

With apologies to Editor David Day, one change was made. It was generally his policy to capitalize the title of his paper, *SOLID*

MULDOON. For the sake of uniformity, it will only be italicized. Also the *The*, which appeared on the masthead, has been dropped for brevity in the text.

Day possessed some unusual ideas about spelling. His spelling has been left as he published it, with an occasional help for the reader.

PROLOGUE

Newspapers, in one form or another, have been published in America since 1704. They have fulfilled a variety of purposes, from reporting the news to arousing readers to action. In the new and emerging west, they were essential for promotion in every way imaginable and for educating, entertaining, and keeping their readers up-to-date. Without one, a community could languish and die; with one, the future looked more promising and substantial than ever.

H. L. Mencken definitely defined what he considered the newspaper's role to be in his own pugnacious manner: "All successful newspapers are ceaselessly querulous and bellicose. They never defend anyone or anything if they can help it; if the job is forced upon them, they tackle it by denouncing someone or something else." The *Chicago Times* agreed with him in 1861. "It is a newspaper's duty to print the news and raise hell."

Writing in a 1787 letter, Thomas Jefferson discussed his view of a newspaper's significance. "The basis of our government being the opinion of the people, the very first object should be to keep that right; and were it left to me to decide whether we should have a government without newspapers, or newspapers without a government, I should not hesitate a moment to prefer the latter."

In defining what his anti-slavery newspaper's policy would be, William Lloyd Garrison wrote in 1831, in *The Liberator* (Boston), "I am in earnest—I will not equivocate—I will not excuse—I will not retreat a single inch; and I will be heard!"

Among his observations on the world around him, Mark Twain, on several occasions, digressed upon the merits of newspapers. "Our own dailies infuriate the reader, pretty often; the German daily only stupefies him." "The old saw says, 'Let a sleeping dog lie.' Still, when there is much at stake it is better to get a newspaper to do it."

It would seem that David Day would have wholeheartedly agreed with most of these remarks and observations. His newspaper, the *Solid Muldoon*, exemplified what a mining camp or town or a Midwestern farm community editor should be doing. Not only did the paper embody the town and surrounding district, but it often represented the best collective memory to preserve what had transpired during the years of its existence.

One of the interesting, rather antiquarian questions that Day definitely did not answer or pass on to the future was how his newspaper's fascinating, yet incongruous, name was derived. In the September 5, 1879 initial issue, he told his readers that "Muldoon" was taken "from the Zulu language;" it meant, according to him, "virgin." Without doubt, this was editor Day "pulling his readers' legs," something he became quite adept and skilled in doing. This practice gained him readers and, at the same time, upset some of the folks he took an editorial swing at.

The following account that came down through the family (probably from his wife Victoria) seems more plausible:

> *His Ouray newspaper partner, Gerald Letcher, asked Day to give their newspaper a name. 'We want a name that means something solid and honest; well something as solid as Bill Muldoon—we'll call it The Solid Muldoon.'*

This selection is accounted for by the "fact that Mr. Day was an admirer of William Muldoon, whom he esteemed as a grand old man of sports, and regarded as the greatest athletic sportsman and promoter of prize fights in New York City."

Dave Day gave another clue in a comment in his August 19, 1882 paper. "William, the original Muldoon, is in Denver."

At the time the *Solid Muldoon* first appeared, a popular song by Ed Harrigan included this verse:

> *For the opposition or politician*
> *Take my word I didn't give a d—n*
> *As I walk the street each friend I meet*
> *Say 'There goes Muldoon—He's a solid man.*

For whatever reason, the name helped set Day's newspaper apart, a fact he no doubt intended—and appreciated.

David Day made his newspaper unique in a number of other ways, as will be seen in the following chapters. Besides being an excellent writer with a good nose for news, Day was controversial, opinionated, conflictive, progressive, the lover of a good argument, reformer, promoter, gad fly, and civic minded. He was all these things and more. In his time, Day became one of the best known Colorado newspapermen, both admired and disliked. There was nothing like a newspaper "war," or a county or town rivalry, or a mining scam to bring the best or the worst out in him. Dave Day loved it all.

He liked to brag and, probably with more than a grain of truth, say that his *Solid Muldoon* had circulation throughout the country. Certainly, Day and "Dayisms" were often quoted. The newspaper and its editor brought notoriety to Ouray, appreciated or not, and a certain amount of fame was awarded its editor.

CHAPTER 1

The Man: David Frakes Day

"**P**ersons attempting to find a motive in this narrative will be prosecuted; persons attempting to find a moral in it will be banished; persons attempting to find a plot in it will be shot." So wrote David Day's older contemporary, Mark Twain, in his classic *Huck Finn*. There exist several early similarities between the two authors and newspapermen; and, in both cases, their humor strikes the heart of later 19th century America. Perhaps, also, Twain's introduction might hold true in what you are about to read.

David Day's early years proved full of trauma, much like Huck's. Typical of rural, pre-Civil War America, he was born on a farm near Cincinnati, Ohio, on March 7, 1847. After his mother died, his "cruel stepmother" insisted that he attend school. Stubbornly deciding not to, he went to live with his grandfather. Apparently, as a Huck Finn prototype, that change of scenery did not satisfy Day. He ran away and "struck out to find liberty and happiness without benefit of schooling."

Meanwhile, as Day wandered about, the country was splitting north and south over such issues as states' rights, slavery, and different economic systems. When war broke out, young Day, in all probability, had not thought very deeply about such matters. However, for whatever reasons, he eventually enlisted in the 57th Ohio Infantry, Company D.

Teenager David Day was a growing boy during the war. When he enlisted on February 1, 1862, at age fifteen, the army report listed him as 5 foot, 5 inches in height. Two years later, when he reenlisted as a veteran, he had grown two inches. In both cases, he was described as having light hair, a light complexion, and blue eyes. Army life benefited him in another way—he improved his reading, writing and spelling. According to his son George, "General A. V. Rice had him (Day) taught to write and spell in order to further increase his usefulness to the army." Memory may have failed Day here. Military records do not list a General A. V. Rice, but there was a General Elliot W. Rice.

The 57th Ohio and its young recruit boarded transports with the rest of the Union army, and then, guarded by gunboats, steamed up the Tennessee River in mid-March. Stopping at Pittsburg Landing, they camped along with what eventually grew to slightly over 37,000 federal troops, all reporting "present for duty." It might have been the most beautiful and pleasant Spring that Day had seen, much warmer than Hamilton County, Ohio; and the Confederate forces did not appear to be anywhere in the neighborhood.

Part of the Army of the Tennessee, the 57th Ohio was in the Third Brigade and the Fifth Division, commanded by Brigadier General William Tecumseh Sherman. Major General Ulysses Grant, the now famed hero who had captured forts Donelson and Henry back in February, commanded the troops. Day had joined a famous army under two of the greatest union generals to emerge during the war.

All had gone well for a while. Detachments of the 57th Ohio carried out reconnaissance, including one trip up river to Eastport, which they found completely abandoned. Another group landed at Chickasaw but found no Confederates. The enemy seemed to have vanished.

Then on a quiet Sunday morning, April 6, the Confederates seemed to attack out of nowhere, and David Day swiftly found out what war was all about. His colonel, Jesse Hildebrandt, described the scene:

> *Early on the morning of Sunday, 6th instant, our pickets were fired on, and shortly after 7 o'clock the enemy appeared in force, presented himself in columns of regiments at least four*

deep. He opened upon our camp a heavy fire from infantry,
which was immediately followed by shell. Having formed my
brigade in line of battle I ordered an advance. The Seventy-
seventh and Fifty-seventh regiments were thrown forward to
occupy a certain position, but encountered the enemy enforce
within 300 yards of our camp. Unfortunately we were not
supported by artillery, and consequently were compelled to
retire under cover to our camp, the engagement becoming
general along the entire front of my command.

Caught completely by surprise, the Union forces retreated,
fought stubbornly, and then retreated almost the entire day through
open fields and into wooded terrain. For a while, the battle swirled
around a beautiful little country church called Shiloh, which meant
in Hebrew ironically, "a meeting place and a sanctuary." By night-
fall, after bitter, desperate fighting, the hard-pressed Federal forces
had stabilized their battlefront. That night steamboats arrived with
desperately needed reinforcements. The next day belonged to the
battered Union troops, as they finally drove the Confederates from
the field, and the battle of Shiloh slipped into history.

Day's baptism in battle had been brutal. The 57th Ohio had
ninety-four men killed, wounded, or captured in what had been
the war's bloodiest battle to date, with northern and southern losses
totaling 3,482 killed, 16,420 wounded, and 3,844 missing. Shocked
northerners and southerners never expected so much carnage, over
23,000 casualties in two days.

Grant put the horror of these two days into perspective when
he wrote:

Shiloh was the severest battle fought at the West during the
war, and but few in the East equaled it for hard, determined
fighting. I saw an open field, in our possession on the second
day, over which the Confederates had made repeated charges

the day before, so covered with dead that it would have been possible to walk across the clearing, in any direction, stepping on dead bodies, without a foot touching the ground.

The Civil War had entered a new phase. Gone was the idea of a one battle war, a negotiated peace, or anything short of total victory. Day seldom spoke publicly about what he had seen or experienced, perhaps realizing it would be hard for those who had not experienced it to grasp the horror.

The devastation at Shiloh brought about a change in attitude. Grant explained as follows:

I gave up all idea of saving the Union except by complete conquest. After this, however, I regarded it as humane to both sides to protect the persons of those found at their homes, but to consume everything that could be used to support or supply armies ... such supplies within the reach of Confederate armies I regarded as much contraband as arms or ordnance stores. Their destruction was accomplished without bloodshed and tended to the same result as the destruction of armies. I continued this policy to the close of the war.

The Civil War had become all encompassing — against troops in the field and civilians at home. It would stay that way. Romantic ideas about warfare, or thoughts of a short conflict, no longer held true.

While not involved in another major battle like the one just fought, Day and his comrades were involved in skirmishes throughout the summer. Such a one came during the evening of June 30, 1862, when they were guarding sixty-seven wagons near Morning Star, Tennessee. When attacked, they fought off the "rebels amid a stampede among the mule teams, many of which became unmanageable and quite a number of wagons were upset." Continuing his report, Colonel William Mungen praised the troops.

I cannot speak too highly of the conduct of the officers and men of the Fifty-seventh Ohio Regiment on that occasion. In short, the entire regiment, or that portion of it present as an escort, could not have behaved better had they been veterans, for every officer and man seemed only anxious to do his duty, and no sign of fear or faltering was exhibited.

Now veteran David Day and his comrades shifted their attention to Vicksburg, Mississippi, the key to reopening the Mississippi River. The only major Confederate stronghold left on the river, this completely fortified "hill city" prevented the splitting of the Confederacy east and west. Vicksburg represented a major military challenge.

Throughout the rest of 1862, the Union Army's attention in the western theater would be focused on this picturesque and charming river town with its ante-bellum homes. Long a major port on the Mississippi River, it now was hailed as the "Gibraltar" of the Confederacy. (Grant might have gotten there sooner, but jealousies and politics, which continually hampered the Union war effort, reared their ugly heads.)

Located on a high bluff that commanded a hairpin bend on the river, the town seemed almost unapproachable except by the north or east. Grant's troops had tried northern approaches unsuccessfully in late 1862. They had even attempted to bypass Vicksburg by trying to divert the river. The troops labored to dig a canal across the peninsula opposite the town, thereby bypassing it and, in theory, leaving the Confederate stronghold "high and dry," so to speak. Everything failed. Grant then threw military theories aside, cut loose from his base, and crossed the Mississippi River. After fighting a series of skirmishes and intense battles, Grant had Vicksburg "completely invested" by May 19.

On May 20 and 21, the Union forces busily strengthened their positions around besieged Vicksburg. Meanwhile, the aggressive

Grant was determined to assault Vicksburg and decided to conduct a combined navy/army attack on May 22. After an all-night bombardment by naval mortars, at dawn 200 guns along Grant's line joined the attack. At 9:30, Admiral David Porter's gunboats and other naval weapons opened fire.

As shells dropped into Vicksburg, the troops prepared for the attack. The noted Civil War historian Shelby Foote wrote: "For the first time in history a major assault was launched by commanders whose eyes were fixed on the hands of watches synchronized the night before. This was necessary in the present case because the usual signal guns would not have been heard above the din of the preliminary bombardment."

Writing in his *Memoirs*, Grant explained the reasons for his attack: "The first consideration of all was: the troops believed they could carry the works in their front, and would not have worked so patiently in the trenches if they had not been allowed to try."

He continued:

> *The attack was ordered to commence on all parts of the line at 10 o'clock A. M. on the 22d with a furious cannonading from every battery in position. All the corps commanders set their time by mine, so that all might open the engagement at the same minute. The attack was gallant, and portions of each of the three corps succeeded in getting up to the very parapets of the enemy, and in planting their battle-flags upon them: but at no place were we able to enter. . . . As soon as it was dark, our troops that had reached the enemy's entrenchments at several points and had been obliged to remain there for security all day, were withdrawn, and thus ended the last assault on Vicksburg.*

Day's commander, Lieutenant-Colonel Samuel R. Mott, 57th Ohio Infantry, in his report of the battle, praised the nine men who had volunteered to lead. Private David Day was one of those men. Of that group, two were killed, two wounded and "the other five, by the aid of Divine Providence, returned to their comrades and regiment." Mott described it further:

> At 10 a. m. we were ordered to fall in [advanced, then halted, by troops in front]. We were again ordered forward, moving as before, the enemy pouring into us a most terrific fire of shot and shell. When within easy range of the works, we were halted and ordered to return the fire of the enemy, which we did; remaining there in line until the following morning, when we were ordered into the position we now hold. . . . Of the conduct of officers and men I can but say they did all that officers and soldiers could do—their whole duty.

A more detailed story appeared in *Deeds of Valor*, a volume describing how men won the Medal of Honor. An amazing fifty-three soldiers from Ohio, Indiana, Missouri, West Virginia, and Illinois infantry regiments were awarded the medal for "bravery and courage" in this battle.

> For superb gallantry and reckless indifference to death and danger, there is nothing in military history to excel the conduct of the 'forlorn hope' that led the general assault on Vicksburg on May 22, 1863. . . .
>
> One hundred and fifty men were required for a "forlorn hope" to lead the general assault and prepare the way for the real attack. As these men would be certain to draw the enemy's fire, there was little probability of any of them returning alive, and on that account it was decided not to order any man to go, but to depend entirely on volunteers. Each regiment was to supply its quota, and in view of the terrible risk to be incurred, orders were given none but unmarried men were to be accepted.

Their assignment was to rush out of a ravine, carrying logs and lumber, and build a bridge over the ditch in front of the fort. Succeeding at that, they then were to plant scaling ladders against the fort's embankment. All the time they would be under the concentrated fire of the Confederate defenders. Once they accomplished everything successfully, the general assault by the Union troops would then follow. If all worked well, Vicksburg would fall.

The moment the "forlorn hope" emerged from the ravine, they came within view of the enemy, who opened so heavy a fire on them that their works were covered with clouds of smoke. The gallant little band advanced at a dead run, but in the eighty rods of open ground which lay between them and the fort, about half of them were shot down. When the survivors arrived at the ditch, they found it impossible to build a bridge, as so many of the logs had been dropped by the way, and it was equally impossible to remain where they were, exposed to the enemy's fire. There was nothing for it but to jump into the ditch and seek shelter.

The other brigades advanced as planned, then stopped, and were driven back by "heavy fire." The attack faltered and failed. The troops then "retired," taking cover as best they could. "All day long, from 10 o'clock in the morning until darkness fell, the unequal fight went on. . . Of the storming party, eighty-five per cent were either killed or dangerously wounded, and few of them escaped without a wound of some kind."

All told, the Union troops had suffered high casualties during their gallant, doomed effort—3,199 had been killed, wounded, or reported missing. For what? They had gained only an appreciation of the strength of the town's defenses. In reality, the volunteers had been sent on a nearly impossible, forlorn mission against long odds. An Illinois colonel called it "the most murderous fire I ever saw."

With the failure of this attack, Grant settled down to a siege of Vicksburg. "I now determined upon a regular siege—to 'out-camp the enemy,' as it were, and to incur no more losses. The experience of the 22d convinced officers and men that this was the best, and they went to work on the defenses and approaches with a will."

Starving, outnumbered, and with no hope of relief by land or water, the beleaguered southern garrison finally surrendered on July 4th. The last remaining Confederate fort on the river capitulated a few days later. The "father of waters" could now again wind its way "unvexed" to the sea. Combined with the northern victory at Gettysburg the day before (July 3), the turning point had been reached in the Civil War with Vicksburg's fall.

Lincoln understood. According to Secretary of the Navy Giddeon Wells, when he told the president the news, the joyful Lincoln threw his arm around his secretary and exclaimed, "I cannot, in words, tell you my joy over this result. It is great, Mr. Wells, it is great!"

From this point on, even after winning the Medal of Honor "for gallantry at Vicksburg, May 22, 1863," David Day's Civil War experience becomes a bit more unclear in the official records. A typical report reads that on December 23, 1863, at Bridgeport, Alabama, he was issued a "list of clothing," including "one pair of Cavalry Pants, two knit shirts, two pair of stockings, and one painted blanket." They tell little, however, about his activities.

Meanwhile, from June 1863 through the rest of the war, except for January and February 1864, when he was "at home on furlough," Day was "absent as orderly on Genl Blairs staff from company D, 57th Reg't Ohio Infantry." His original company, in the meantime, mustered out. However, because Day had enlisted later, he, at that time, was "not eligeable [sic]" until February 2, 1864. Promptly, on the second, he reenlisted as a "veteran volunteer" in his old regiment. At this point, the government records go silent as to what he might have been doing or where he was during the remainder of the war.

Years later (1942), his family loaned personal family material to the author of an article on Day published in *Pioneers of the San Juan*

Country. The records stated he became chief of scouts for General Frank P. Blair when he was seventeen years old. Among his adventures, he "was four times wounded by bullets and was cut through the right foot with a saber." Furthermore, Day was "three times a prisoner under sentence of death." When he was first captured, he was "taken to the terrible Andersonville prison in Georgia, August 4, 1864."

He fortunately did not stay in this "hell hole" too long. Escaping on September 7, Day was then, as written in *Pioneers of the San Juan Country*:

> *recaptured by blood-hounds near Social Circle, Georgia on the 17th; he was taken to a Confederate prison at Florence, South Carolina, Oct. 3, escaped Oct. 7, and reached the Federal lines at Rome, Georgia, Oct. 17, 1864.*

How did he accomplish this?

> *Day had a fairly good suit of Confederate uniform and traveled as a member of the 16th Carolina Infantry. . . . He passed through Confederate lines and walked to Rome, Georgia.*

Day wrote about his experiences occasionally in the *Muldoon*. Reminiscencing about those days in the July 6, 1883 edition, and prompted by a reunion of "Gen. Sherman's battle scarred veterans," he recalled, "July 4th, 1863, the stars and stripes waved over Vicksburg. On the 31st of July '64, Ouray's distinguished Colonel was provided with an escort and free pass to Andersonville. Sad Day the 31st for the Union Cause." That was the only time in the first six and a half years of the *Muldoon* that he mentioned his Civil War experiences.

Though he had never attained the rank of colonel while in service, he had reached that "honorary" rank in the Colorado

National Guard, as a member of the governor's "staff." Appointed on February 12, 1883, as an Aide-de-Camp to Governor James B. Grant, he served until February 26, 1885, when the new Republican Governor, Benjamin Eaton, chose not to reappoint him. Considering his political partisanship, that decision was completely understandable.

Back in the war, Day and twenty-one others later were captured in a fight at Fayetteville, North Carolina. They were then imprisoned, but all soon escaped as the war neared its end. Reporting on this campaign, Major General O. O. Howard provided the details of what happened amid the rain and roads that were like "quicksand."

> *Captain William Duncan, with the scouts, went ahead rapidly toward Fayetteville, and succeeded in securing the bridge over Little Rockfish from being destroyed by the rebel cavalry. Early the next morning, March 11, I directed him to take all the available mounted men at my headquarters and scout toward Fayetteville. He encountered the enemy's pickets just outside the town, which he drove before him easily, but on entering the town he met a large force of the enemy's cavalry. The scouts were driven back, and Captain Duncan was captured. He afterward escaped, and reports that he was stripped of everything valuable in the presence of [Lt. General Wade] Hampton and [Major General Matthew] Butler.*

The bitterness of these last days of the war comes through clearly in this report, particularly a story about Hampton killing a captive union soldier.

While David Day was not mentioned, Howard did commend "the services of Captain Duncan . . . in the way of reconnoitering and scouting have been invaluable to me." Maj. General Frank Blair and the Seventeenth Corps also were there which lends further support to the fact that Day was in the vicinity. Further, Howard noted,

"I can say that in pursuit of the insurgent army from Goldsborough to Raleigh and beyond the same energy and cheerful conduct as ever before were witnessed."

Day was mustered out August 14, 1865, at Little Rock, Arkansas. He was still owed $190 of his original $400 bonus. Greatly admiring his commander, he followed him to Missouri. St. Louis lawyer, politician, and later Civil War general, Frank Blair had joined the Republican party and helped build a strong pro-union organization in the midst of a countryside packed with Democrats and southern sympathizers. While Day had been scouting, Major General Blair had campaigned with Sherman on his march from Atlanta to the sea.

Day settled in Marshall, Saline County, where his parents had moved just before the war. Named after Chief Justice John Marshall, the town had been established in 1839, and it and the county had gained a measure of fame for its salt deposits. Santa Fe traders "stocked up" on salt here for use during their journey over the famous trail.

During the Civil War, the "battle of Marshall" had swirled around the town and throughout the surrounding countryside. On October 13, 1863, while Day busily scouted farther east, some 3,000 Union and Confederate cavalry fought a daylong skirmish (locals liked to call it a battle) before the defeated southerners retreated to Arkansas, with the northern forces in "hot" pursuit.

All that aside, Day initially clerked in a store, "for a Jewish merchant," where he encountered Victoria Sophia Folck. She recalled those courting days in *Pioneers of the San Juan Country*, while at the same time telling us much about herself:

> I went to the store to buy a pair of shoes. He tried the shoes
> on my feet; they suited me and I bought them. Soon after that
> Mr. Day and a friend called on me one evening. At that time
> I was engaged to one man who had money, for three years;

and to two others all at the same time; but I was just flirting with the whole outfit. The first time I saw Mr. Day I thought, I will marry him.

There was, however, a problem.

But I was a Southern girl and he was a hated Northerner and my family opposed the idea. I flirted with him and broke the engagement. He was desperate and said he would go jump in the river We made up and were married at Arrow Rock, March 10, 1870.

Marshall's *Saline County Weekly Progress* carried the wedding announcement in its March 18 edition:

MARRIED

In Arrow Rock, on the evening of the 10th last, by elder William Henry Robinson, Mr. David Day to Miss Victoria Folck.

Our best benediction attend the happy couple in all their trials and vexations of life. In the midst of all their gayety and exuberance of joy, they did not forget us; they sent us a bottle of grape juice. Ah, the wine! The wine! One sip of it raised our drooping spirits, and in good feeling, placed us beyond the 'bliss of dreams.

A charivari (noisy mock serenade) promptly "honored" the young couple, Victoria continued. "The boys serenaded us that night with their band. They were the *loveliest* boys. I had five gallons of wine and plenty of cake and we all had a great time."

The Days entered married life "in a beautiful little cottage nicely furnished." Over the next twelve years, five children would enlarge the family. Two more would be born later in Colorado, but they would die in early childhood. "Mr. Day, meanwhile, entered the grocery business." Being the structured Victorian age, Victoria always referred to her husband as Mr. Day when discussing him in public.

Victoria had a bit of a problem cooking, which she honestly admitted, and, also a temper:

> *I didn't do so well at cooking—the first time I made biscuits, Mr. Day said, 'If I was to go down town now, I'd never get back, these biscuits are so heavy. I wanted to learn to cook, and I particularly wanted to make a good light bread. The first time I tried it, I put my sponge under the stove to rise and went over to sister Mattie's. When I came back to work it into loaves, there I found my neighbor's cat asleep on the sponge. I took that cat by the tail and I went outside where my neighbor could see me, and I warped that cat up against the side of the house as hard as I could several times; then I threw out the bread. That cat never came back again.*

The Days were not among the "movers and shakers" of their community. Therefore, they did not make the news very often. Dave Day did serve as an election judge in a city election held in April, 1874. They must also have read the not uncommon news of their town and of county neighbors who were going to Colorado. Even some mining news occasionally made its way into the paper. It reported "on good authority," for example, on March 4, 1870, that a silver lode had been discovered in Wayne County, Missouri, though it was much more famous for its lead mines.

As Day read his local newspaper, he gained some ideas about the business of promotion. For one thing, as an editor you promoted your local town, its citizenry, and the county; particularly if your paper hoped to gain advertising, circulation, and a favorable public readership. Again, to turn to the March 4, 1870 issue, the editor rhapsodized about Saline County. "In natural bounty—all that is necessary to secure to our people material and social greatness—Saline County is unsurpassed by another extent of territory in the world."

To make up for his lack of formal education, Day "studied," an undefined term, but there was no question from his later life that he gained both a practical and "scholarly" education. During this time, he also wrote "anonymously for local newspapers," starting his career in the field.

His hometown newspaper, the four-page *Weekly Progress,* was ardently Democratic in its leanings, since newspapers generally

Dave Day in his younger years.
Courtesy of Denver Public Library.

tended to be quite passionately political in the late 19th century. As might be expected, this southern newspaper was also anti-Black and ardently anti-radical Republican because of their support of the Blacks. Each issue included poetry, and some humor. National news came first, followed by local items, and there were those always present advertisements. In this respect, the *Progress* proved similar to its other small town contemporaries.

Despite his admiration for Frank Blair, Dave Day, sometime along the way, became an active Democrat, a not unusual development for Missouri. Feelings ran strong after the Civil War about abolitionists and radical Republicans throughout the South. Missouri proved no exception. For example, a meeting was announced for "Saline County Citizens" in the *Weekly Progress* (February 4, 1868):

> For the opponents of oppressive taxation, negro supremacy, radical dishonesty, bigotry, and misrule generally, the times are indeed auspicious. We are not prepared to renew the contest under much more favorable circumstances. . . . a final assault against the forces of negro-worshiping fanatics and public plunderers along the entire line.

Day might have been a Democrat, but he never showed such strong racial attitudes in his later writings.

Being ambitious, Day had left his clerking position and opened a grocery store. Despite his ambitions, he ran into a problem. Quoting Victoria: "Mr. Day was doing well in a grocery business when he lost his modest savings and interests through endorsement of a note for a friend."

He was now determined to join those thousands of others who had decided to start anew in that land of opportunity, the West. He had selected Colorado. Dave Day arrived in the new mining town of Ouray, located at the northern end of the promising San Juan Mining District, early in 1878. To temporarily maintain and tide himself over, he chopped wood for a living.

A Missouri friend of his, lawyer Gerald Letcher, likewise journeyed west to Ouray. He knew of Day's dabbling in newspaper writing (Day had written unsigned articles for the local paper) and "thought he had talent." Letcher heard of a paper for sale in neighboring Lake City and joined with some fellow Ouray Democrats to purchase it. According to Day's son, George Vest Day, his enthusiastic father "tramped twenty-eight miles on foot to Lake City, bought the printing outfit and shipped it by wagon over the long road to Ouray."

Victoria and the children stayed home, while husband and father ventured into the "wild west." She recounted her adventures, when she finally decided to join her husband:

> *In September 1881, I left Marshall with four babies—and the littlest one was sick—and started West to join Mr. Day. . . . When the train stopped at Pueblo at 4 P. M. I was so tired that I didn't even make a move to get off. 'Madam,' said the conductor 'you'll have to get off.'*
>
> *[She and children got off] While we were crossing the tracks a train pulled in and Mr. Day swung off right in front of me. He took us to a hotel.*
>
> *At two o'clock in the morning our train pulled out for Gunnison; the babies had been bathed and the laundry had been done by a Chinaman. The train was full of miners— they were so good to us—they gave up their seat so the babies could have places to sleep.*
>
> *. . . We got to Montrose about the middle of the afternoon and stayed long enough to get a doctor and medicine for the babies [two now sick]. He was an Army doctor with General MacKenzie and soldiers stationed there.*
>
> *'Say, madam, are these all yours?' asked the doctor— 'Well, you must have had 'em as fast as you could get them!' 'You bet I did! I said.'*

Husband Dave put the following comment in the *Muldoon* (September 9, 1881). "Sunday the '*Muldoon* man' will leave for Pueblo, go meet his wife and babes, and it behooves us to state that simultaneously with her arrival there will be a 'dreadful fall off in picnics and such like.' Reform is inevitable."

Portrait photograph of Victoria Day, later in life.
Center of Southwest Studies, Fort Lewis College

They stayed in Ouray for three years. With his usual sense of humor, Day announced in the August 29, 1884, issue that his wife and family were going back east for a visit.

> *Mrs. D. F. Day and the little ones will leave to-morrow for the east—the madam to visit relatives and friends, and the little ones to attend school. During their absence we shall devote our leisure to looking after the widows and such others of the opposite sex as may feel in need of spirited consolation. Office first room to the left over Carnay's tonsorial emporium. Come early and avoid the rush.*

The support for his family depended on the *Muldoon's* success. David Day also had a trait that promised to help him in the newspaper business, bravery. He had displayed that repeatedly during the war at Shiloh, Vicksburg, and elsewhere, and his wife Victoria summed up this attribute: "Mr. Day wasn't afraid of anyone or anything—he wasn't afraid of the Devil! He did not know what fear was. Although his life was at stake he was not in the habit of carrying a gun."

She recounted one episode when he came home "later than usual, [and] looked a little nervous." Victoria asked if there was anything wrong, to which Dave replied, "'Oh, nothing,' ate his supper and retired." Later she found that he had been shot at and "the bullet had gone through his hat."

He had a great sense of humor, even about himself. Writing in his *Solid Muldoon*, March 7, 1884, editor Day told his readers. "This being the 7th day of March, the *Muldoon* tragedian is 37 years old. Donations will be received upon until 12 midnight, currency, provisions, stimulants, old clothes, pool chips, etc. received."

The man, the town, and the newspaper now had all come together. At this moment, the future was up to David Frakes Day. As Henry David Thoreau had written in his classic, "Walden," in 1854, "What a man thinks of himself, that it is which determines, or rather, indicates, his fate."

CHAPTER 2

The Paper

What significance did a newspaper have to a mining camp and district? The *Dolores News* (September 23, 1879) vigorously, and in no uncertain terms, told its readers: "A mining camp without a newspaper is indeed a flat and insipid place." Furthermore, it said that the "outside world can have but little knowledge of its existence and the owners of its mines have no hope but to remain in a state of masterly inactivity always waiting for something to turn up." The paper promised to "strive energetically, faithfully and truthfully to publish" features about the "mines and mining in the San Juan country."

Not finished, the editor, John Curry, went on, soaring into editorial rhetoric. "A live newspaper in a mining camp is worth to it millions of dollars. It gives it 'stability.'" The *News* would be the "medium by which the world would learn of the existence, growth and prosperity of Rico and the pioneer mining district." In addition, when the camp "begins to show signs of being unable to sustain a newspaper" there "is no surer indication of decay. From that day forward the camp flickers and dies out." Curry would know how true that was as he moved around the San Juan editing five or six newspapers along the way.

What did a newspaper mean to a particular community? Almost universally, the first issue of the paper tried to explain that and justify its coming, its objectives, and its plans for future existence.

In the initial issue, the editor of Lake City's *Silver World* (June 19, 1875) informed his readers of the newspaper's optimistic goals. "We shall preach no sermons and shall not dabble in politics." Also, there "will be nothing pressing upon our time or space to prevent giving full and complete reports from this and the adjacent mining districts."

What the editor planned to do was —"supply the San Juan Country" with a paper "which might be its exclusive representative."

The *Ouray Times* explained its intentions prominently in the paper's initial issue, June 16, 1877. "A good paper is a great value to a town and the surrounding country all admit." Henry C. Olney, the editor, went on to explain that he "felt" the "need for some medium through which the world outside could be informed of what was being done here." He also "wanted to aid in the development of the riches which are locked up in these mountains."

Caroline Romney arrived in booming Durango in December, 1880, to start its pioneer newspaper, the *Durango Record*. In what was considered a man's world, she more than held her own as an editor, news gatherer, writer, reformer, and town "gadfly." She emphatically told her readers what she intended to do, along with a few Victorian flourishes.

> *In making its first appearance on the shores of Time, the* Durango Record *will be expected in accordance with custom, to give some account of itself, some reason for its being. Nature abhors a vacuum, the* Record *therefore took form to fill the void in the newspaper field existing at Durango. The city needed a paper; therefore the* Record.
>
> *First and foremost, it will be devoted to Durango and its interests and service. It will also afford a permanent record of the growth and prosperity of the town from its earliest days and prove a faithful ally in the furtherance of its future development.*
>
> *Next to the town, the* Record *owes allegiance to southwestern Colorado, a land not only 'flowing with milk and honey,' but seamed with silver and gold and floored with coal.*

Politically, Caroline Romney would be foursquare Republican "whose policy has been so triumphantly vindicated both by the abundant prosperity of our country and the voice of her contented people at the polls."

In these new camps, editors faced problems that might have stymied their eastern contemporaries. First and highly important was that a newspaper needed to get in on the ground floor of its community's existence, and it certainly proved equally vital to the camp and district to have its promotional outlet in place. The editor of Rico's *Dolores News*, for example, arrived in the camp, in July 1879, "before a half dozen log huts received dirt coverings and not a house with a roof on it in the new town of Rico."

In the August 28 issue, the rest of the story appeared. A lot had been secured and arrangements made to erect an office, "but progress has been slow." Thus, the first issues appeared from a tent. There were, its editor explained:

> *no tables, desk or chairs to be had, no conveniences save a log divided in half with smooth sides turned up and laid over four upright pieces stuck into the ground. A candle box served for an easy chair and a soap and cigar box or two hold the loose papers.*

Nothing stopped the press, and the *News* appeared, much to the delight of the few local readers.

The *Dolores News* (August 28, 1879) welcomed the *Muldoon*, an "uncommon name for a newspaper." It "pops the individual who takes it up and opens its folds, like a little shock of the electric battery. . ." and "sticks to mind, indelible and fixed like plaster to a poor man's ribs." Editor Curry, a staunch Republican, went on to welcome his new rival and wish "it every success outside of politics" that "are possible for a live, genuine wide-awake and up and doing newspaper."

Curry did not know what he wished for, or he might have been much less congratulatory. Now, dear reader, as newspaper men and women were wont to say, let us turn center stage over to David F. Day and his *Solid Muldoon*. While the newspaper's official title was *The Solid Muldoon*, editor Day seldom used the whole phrase, dropping "the." That policy will also be followed in reference to the title.

Initial editor, and eventual owner, Day expressed some clearly defined ideas as to what a newspaper should accomplish. The "old" veteran wrote what he called "General Order No. 4" in his September 30,1881 *Muldoon*.

> *It is a matter of sublime insignificance to us what certain individuals in this village say about 'Dave Day and his* Muldoon.' *David runs this* Muldoon *strictly in accordance with the dictates of his own conscience—runs it in the interests of Ouray county and that portion of her people who are HONEST.*
>
> *We declined, several months since, to enter into the ignominious work of white-washing schemers and scoundrels, and we shall hardly consent, at this stage of the game, to deprive the rising generation of our example. What we have to say we SAY, and assert it in language that permits of but one construction.*
>
> *During the two years we have been conducting the exercises in this* Muldoon *we have never wronged, maligned, or misrepresented one single individual, female or male, through its columns. When we characterize an individual as either a scoundrel, or a thief the credentials are invariably in our keeping, and the silence, with which the accused submit, is proof positive of guilt. It has always been our desire to get along smoothly and nicely with this people, but if the good will and lasting friendship of a few scheming and treacherous scalawags are to be purposed at the price of ignoration [sic] and ostracism of a class of our citizens who are morally*

and socially their peers, you can count us out. We ask those backbiting friends to come to the front with their wrongs and woes—meet us as we meet you—frankly and openly.

In conclusion allow us to assure you that in the future, as in the past, we shall not hurt the good by sparing the bad. This is all.

A man of decided opinions, Day printed a piece in the October 17, 1879 *Muldoon* that described what an editor should not do in and with his paper. In all likelihood, this was a "boiler plate" article that he "borrowed" from some other newspaper.

1. Publish communications without knowing the name of the author.

2. Puff church fairs free and pay your way through like a little man.

3. Say of each candidate for office, 'if elected, he will make a popular and efficient officer.'

4. Try to make the paper reflect every whim and fancy of the public.

. . .

6. Every body knows how to run a newspaper, take everybody's advice.

. . .

11. Do not forget to state 'Bunker' is feeling as big as a Dutch barn—it's a boy and weighs nine pounds.

. . .

13. Wish all newly married couples, 'many years of wedded bliss.'

14. Call all social gatherings or parties 'the event of the season.'

15. Follow these rules for three years and if you don't die of grief and disappointment, call and receive a chromo.

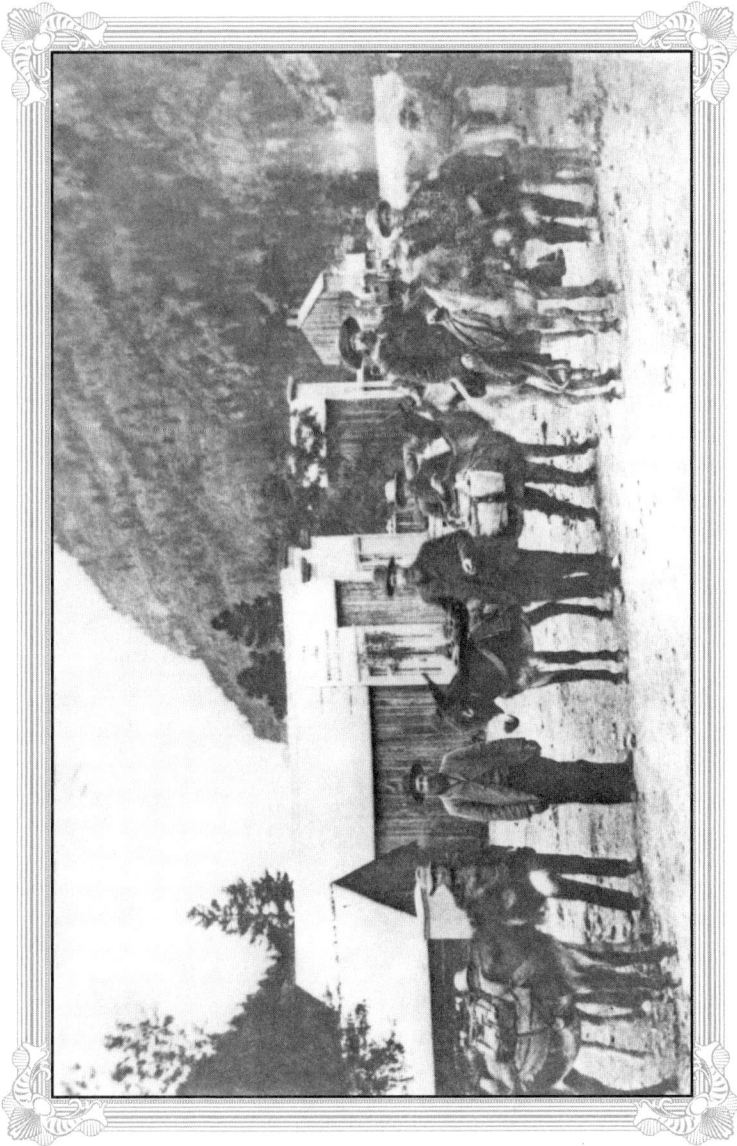

Henry Ripley (man with burro at the center) was Ouray's first newspaper publisher.
Ruth and Marvin Gregory Collection

Letting the editor speak further for himself, something Dave seemed never to be against doing, tells us much about the man and his journalistic ideas. He ardently believed his paper, among other things, must defend and promote Ouray and attack any rivals who dared challenge it, or its mines, and even the county. A classic example appeared in the January 23, 1883 issue. Neighboring San Juan County and Silverton loomed in the sights of his editor's "gun" this issue, just like Johnny Reb twenty years before when he campaigned through the South.

> *We expect the Silverton papers to keep up appearances, as they have done since the camp started—by repeated and inconsistent lying . . .*
> *'Ouray vs. San Juan County'*
> *Ouray combines mining, grazing and agriculture.*
> *San Juan combines charcoal, wrecked smelters and gall.*
> *Ouray offers the miner choice between Denver, Pueblo, Gunnison, Salt Lake, and Omaha ore buyers.*
> *San Juan, an indifferent usurious, pay-you-next week home market.*
> *Ouray has good mountain roads, hot springs, school houses, churches and water works.*
> *San Juan drinks branch water, summer whiskey and educates the rising generation at the dance houses and other dens of iniquity.*

His son George Vest Day remembered one of his father's quotes about some of Day's fellow editors. "God hates a coward, yet there are several of them engineering so called newspapers." In the 19th century rough and tumble newspaper world, Day more than held his own.

David Day could not be said to have been unusual in his outspokenness and editorial stands or his haranguing of individuals or schemes. He just proved more readable, more controversial, more quotable, and possessed of a greater "damn the torpedoes' attitude than many of his contemporaries. Nor was he one who would back off from a fight. Feisty and full of "vim and vigor" might describe him to a fare-thee-well. Thus, thanks to its editor, the *Solid Muldoon* became famous in its day.

CHAPTER 3

The Town

Optimistic, and probably excited, David Day arrived in the mining community of Ouray, located at the northern end of the San Juan mining district, where he would eventually start a newspaper. In one of the most beautiful spots in Colorado, Ouray was a relative youngster at the moment. A youngster, yes, but one that set out to prove from the start that it belonged in the urban world of Victorian America.

Named after Queen Victoria, this era stressed genteel refinement, high morality, the home, the sacredness of women and children, sentimentality, and a religious overtone to life. Mining communities strived to live up to these goals but found, like other American communities and Americans in general, this hard to do in the materialistic, fast changing, profit seeking, and often hedonistic world about them. The image confirmed one thing; the substance quite another.

The little mining camp of Ouray first arrived on the scene in 1876 as the San Juan mining rush evolved from prospecting into development. Over Ute objections (after all, this had been their land for centuries), prospectors had reached the valley as early as 1861. By the first part of 1870s, as the San Juan mining rush resumed, permanent settlement followed.

Isolated from much of the rest of the region by the towering San Juan mountains that encircled it, Ouray opened to the north, where the beautiful Uncompahgre Valley awaited settlers. Since that was the gateway through which the initial miners and other settlers arrived, it meant that they had to travel through the Ute reservation to reach the budding community.

Ouray, one of the fortunate mining camps, evolved quickly into a town. Therefore, it did not languish and eventually decline as its mines failed to match expectations or proved to have low grade, pocket deposits. One factor that certainly helped was the first state legislature creating Ouray County, in January 1877, with Ouray as the county seat. While growth was not overwhelmingly fast for this mining community, the 1880 census taker counted 864 residents, which proved better than many contemporaries. Then matters improved with additional mining development and the eventual appearance of the railroad. The 1890 figure nearly tripled to over 2,500 ten years later. Part of that rapid growth can be attributed to the removal of the neighboring Uncompahgre Utes.

At one time, all the area had been Ute land, but the 1873 Brunot Agreement had opened the San Juan Mountains, from future Ouray south to the future Durango, to onrushing settlers and miners. That agreement never really satisfied the new Coloradans who wanted their northern neighbors out, nor the Utes who wished to hunt and travel in the San Juans as they had for generations. The "Utes Must Go" headline in the first issue of the *Ouray Times* emphatically stated and clearly exhibited the feelings of Coloradans. The killing of agent Nathan Meeker and others in September, 1879, proved to be a pivotal event; and, within two years, the Utes were gone.

At last, freight wagons and settlers did not have to cross the Ute reservation when coming to Ouray by the easiest and fastest way through that northern gateway. Now the miners, mining communities, and the whole region gained the freedom to settle, to prosper and to develop the land and natural resources without "threatening" neighbors. This epitomized the great American dream that had drawn pioneers westward since Jamestown, Virginia in 1607.

Meanwhile, the mining town of Ouray had gained specialized businesses such as meat markets, clothiers, drug stores, and groceries, while neighboring mining camps in their smaller business districts had general merchants, a saloon or two, and perhaps a restaurant or boarding house. Ouray also had more lawyers, doctors, saloons, and proudly boasted a better school system, hospital, and

The Town of Ouray about 1882 taken from the
Mineral Farm Mine. No. 1530
Ouray Historical Society

more newspapers than its neighboring camps. For example, the *Times*, on August 28, 1879, as the *Solid Muldoon* neared its debut, waxed excitedly over it. Ouray's business district contained one each of a bakery, blacksmith shop, watchmaker, bank, meat market, and gunsmith, as well as drug, dry goods, general merchandise, and hardware stores. Two groceries and hotels, three real estate offices, four saloons, and six lawyers completed the mix.

With Ouray starting to come into its own, that total could be compared to Animas Forks. This camp, located high up in the mountains along the Animas River, contained only one each of a general merchandise store, hotel, meat market, blacksmith, and miners' supply store. Even its summer population grew to no more than a couple of hundred. When winter arrived, many of its citizens departed.

The smaller camps, such as Red Mountain, Ironton, and Animas Forks fell into the economic orbit of the larger towns that fought tooth and nail when some interloper threatened to take away their business. Ouray would fight, especially with Silverton, with such aggressive behavior.

Mining towns also had a certain "attitude" about them that a camp might try to emulate but had not the wherewithal to maintain. For example, a proud resident explained to the *Ouray Times*, July 14, 1877, that twelve months ago Ouray had only a few dozen cabins and about 100 inhabitants. But today:

> its principal streets are lined on either side by large and substantial business houses representing every line of traffic and inland commerce. Everywhere within the city limits can be seen neat and handsome dwelling houses.
>
> [Furthermore the population] is quiet and orderly, and intelligent and enterprising.
>
> The rapidity which school houses and church organizations have recently been established shows evidence of a

good moral tone of the citizens and a high appreciation for
those divine and intellectual attainments so well calculated
to enlighten and adorn the mind and elevate and expand the
faculties of the soul.

Even putting aside Victorian sentimentality, pride, and morality, this quote illustrates the rapid evolution of Ouray and its determination to grow into a typical Victorian age community.

Mining towns, and many mining camps, did not relish the law-
less image so often given to them in the Eastern press. In order
to attract visitors, settlers, and investors, they had to prove to the
world that they were like their urban counterparts across the country, in areas such as refinement, law and order, churches, schools,
businesses, and quality folk.

Ouray had hardly started when jealousy reared its head. Lake
City's *Silver World* headlined a May 13, 1876 article, "Expose the
Fraud!" The article went on to state that the road into the camp
(Ouray) was almost "impassible, and lined with dead animals and
wagons turned over." Not finished, the *World* then called its rival an
"unmitigated fraud and humbug."

After those blasts, the *Times* responded. "We do not publish
statements with any desire to mar the prospects and the prosperity
of the struggling hamlet across the range." It was a "simple matter
of justice to the many" who were liable to be "misled by rose tinted
stories so industriously circulated to the outside world."

Welcome to the world of a mining community. It was no-holds-
barred jealousy and on-going feuds. Long before Day arrived, the
battle had been joined. In this world of "survival of the fittest,"
every mining town needed to have its newspaper be its guardian
and counter attacker.

A defender, yes; a watchdog, definitely. For example, at home,
Day would editorialize about and the city trustees would wres-
tle with an assortment of local problems. In October, 1883, the

trustees passed an ordinance relating to "gambling, keeping gambling, bawdy and disorderly houses" within the corporate limits and three miles beyond. Depending on the offense, a fine system of $5 to $300 was established. The ordinance even went so far as to allow all marshals and police officers "in executing their duties to break open doors for the purpose of taking possession of gambling devices and all persons having such gambling devices without complaint or warrant."

This might have looked good on paper—and pleased Victorian sensibilities—but, in reality, it threatened one of the reasons for a mining community's existence. In the male-dominated mining world, drinking, gambling and visiting the "fair but frail" (who shockingly practiced "fornication," according to part IV of the ordinance) provided one of the main reasons to come down from the nearby mines to visit the "city." The choice remained plain: offer the red-light district as an attraction or watch business and customers go elsewhere.

The theoretical solution was the ordinance, but the practical answer was simply to let unseemly businesses flourish and collect fines while looking the other way. Also, the fines fattened the city coffers. All this caught Dave Day's rigorous eye as shall be discussed in several subsequent chapters.

Businesses in Ouray, like other mining communities, had to purchase licenses, according to ordinances. Collecting the license fees presented an ongoing problem, particularly among saloon operators. Then there persisted the emotional and often taxpayer issues of city expenses. In April, 1883, the trustees set the annual appropriations for the coming year at slightly over $23,000, which included $1,369 for the police and $9,305 for the fire departments. Crusader Day always had an editorial pen ready to point out whether Ouray really received its money's worth. In his eyes, it sometimes did not.

The condition of city streets caught the public's, the editor's and the council's attention repeatedly. In June of 1882, to illustrate, sixty-two taxpayers requested that "2nd Avenue be graded at a cost not exceeding $400." The council agreed.

The next year, in November, sixty-five citizens called attention "to the fact that the streets and alleys are in a very filthy condition." They went further, stating that a "large amount of decaying vegetable and animal matter" was thrown out of a certain hotel, "causing an intolerable stench and breeding contagious diseases." The councilmen promptly instructed the marshal to "keep a barrel or box at back doors (of all businesses) to put all refuge in." Further adding to his responsibilities, the marshal was "to see that it (each box or barrel) is drawn away every week."

Ouray's town government was typical for the era—a mayor, recorder, and four trustees, plus a town treasurer, attorney, and a variety of committees of three members each, all trustees. They met "regularly on the first and third Mondays of each month at 8 pm," and reporter Dave Day watched them like a hawk.

They faced a variety of issues that might include purchasing new fire hoses or a carriage, "social evils," or putting "manure" around fire hydrants to keep them from freezing. When smallpox broke out in neighboring Montrose, in May of 1883, Ouray's mayor appointed a "select committee" to contact doctors and make "arrangements to have everybody vaccinated and have doctors go to the schools to have all children vaccinated." Another committee looked into selecting "a cabin to be used as a pest house providing small pox breaks out."

Much as Dave Day would later do, the *Ouray Times* occasionally chastised its readers. On December 1, 1877, its editor wrote a piece on "how to kill a town." His salient points were:

> *Put up more houses than you are obliged to occupy.*
> *Rent empty buildings for three times their value.*
> *Take several New York and Chicago papers but not your own town paper.*

*Or if you do, always manage to be about three years behind
with your subscription.*
*Turn cold shoulders to every businessman who seeks home
among you.*
*Look at all newcomers with a scowl of suspicion, particularly
if he or she does not attend your church or is not of your
political belief.*

Tourism and the value of the hot springs also sat on the editor's
agenda. When the hot springs were inspected by an agent of the
state board of health (September, 1877), he "is very much pleased
with them." Much to the joy of the paper and locals, he continued
to point out how "very valuable" the springs were "to treat some
diseases especially rheumatism," a common complaint.

Those characteristics encouraged the editor, who noted "these
springs will prove of great value to our town." They would, he
believed, "bring us many persons suffering from diseases to which
they [springs] are adapted to cure." Before becoming a health
mecca, and a popular nineteenth-century enticement, however, he
cautioned his readers "their benefit will not be so soon apparent"
as a "good mine."

Despite the paper's boosterism, the *Times* would take the town
government to task. It was a positive step forward to have the street
supervisor digging and blasting numerous "large and unsightly
stumps" on the streets. But, for nearby business houses and resi-
dences, "it is a dangerous business." One stump "barely missed" the
front of a store, the paper reported, and the practice had become a
"dangerous business" that "may prove expensive" for the city.

Like western mining communities elsewhere, Ouray desired to
emulate Eastern and Midwestern towns in architecture and in every
other respect possible. When it came to physical appearance, that
meant replacing log structures with frame buildings and then, as
quickly as possible, frame with brick. A sawmill arrived in 1876,

and, by June of the next year, a brickyard was started "about a mile below town." The *Times* promptly challenged its readers, "who will have the honor of erecting the first brick building?" Not only would this enhance the appearance of the town, it would impress visitors and investors with an air of permanency and faith in the future. As the writer pointed out, this would "cost but little, if any greater, than for log or frame buildings." Also, it would hopefully provide more protection from that great fear of mining communities—the "fire scourge."

It was not only architecture they hoped to copy. Ourayites, and their contemporaries throughout the mining West, wanted to show the world that Victorian society had arrived. The *Times* in the July 21, 1877 issue, praised the "Cornet band." A "good brass band is a handy thing to have round," and "we hope musicians in town will take hold and make this band one of the best in the state." Local pride was always at stake, whether it involved a band or a baseball team. The ever-popular fraternal lodges also came, as did a debate over women's suffrage that Coloradans turned down in an election that year. One of the main advocates of the cause, Susan B. Anthony, was supposed to speak in Ouray in September, but, to the disappointment of a "large number of people who were quite anxious to hear her," she was prevented from making her appearance by a mountain storm.

One factor, and only one, in Ourayites' eyes at least, remained missing. Ouray dreamed of becoming the heart and soul of the development and growth of the "amazing and unlimited" potential of San Juan mining. To achieve that, it had to gain a railroad connection. The railroad represented the ultimate in transportation in post-Civil War America—the fastest, most comfortable, all-weather, and cheapest way to get from here to there. A community without one symbolized a dead community, indeed.

The railroad reached Colorado in 1870. Denver secured three lines that summer and felt it had come of age as the "queen of the mountains and plains." No mining district, after the California gold rush and the Comstock's first bonanza, really hit full stride until the railroad arrived, a fact the San Juaners knew. For them, the greatest hope lay with William Jackson Palmer's Denver & Rio Grande, Colorado's "baby railroad."

When it reached its new "metropolis" Durango in 1881, it looked like the long awaited savior had arrived. The next year the railroad steamed into Silverton, just across the mountains from Ouray. Those, however, were some of the highest, most rugged, and often snow-bound mountains in the whole United States. Much to the dismay of Ouray, the community continued to sit on the outside looking on, as urban rivals gained the iron horse. Yet, all its boosters could do – and continue to do – was look north and hope that the D&RG would eventually chug south through the valley from Montrose.

Despite a promising start, Ouray found itself caught in economic doldrums within a few months of its birth. In spite of the fact that some folks believed that the new mining district and town would not be affected by national economic developments, that proved not to be the case. The crash of 1873 that evolved into a national depression by the time Ouray appeared on the scene lingered on as Ouray struggled through its first years. An editorial in the *Times* (September 15, 1877) finally admitted that the situation was real. Its author, however, did manage to make Ouray's problems seem less dire by pointing the finger at neighboring Lake City as being even in worse shape:

> *Talk about business being dull! Just go over to Lake City and see the long-drawn out countenances of the business men, hear their complaints, notice all the works shut down, and then quit growling about dull times here. It is public talk over there that not a mine in the district is paying expenses. Many of our mines are, and shipping to Lake City at that.*

If the railroad represented a boom and high expectations for development to Ouray, it proved equally important, or more so, to its economic pillar, mining. Neither the scenery, as spectacular as it was, nor the hot springs, as inviting as they were, summoned many people to Ouray and the San Juan Mountains. They would eventually serve as enticements, but not at the moment. Mining and the beckoning lure of getting "rich without working" brought the desired number of miners, prospectors, investors, and settlers.

Prospects, which in the owners' eyes represented "mines," could be found almost at the edge of town and scattered about the surrounding mountains, east, south, and west. Even such a rival as Lake City tipped its hat to Ouray—the mines "about Ouray are all looking well and giving good results to their owners" (August, 1876).

Because the district opened later than Silverton or Lake City, Ouray trailed a step or two behind them in promotion and development. That hardly slowed locals. Not being a placer, or free gold district, where the metal gleamed in the streams, Ouray miners quickly dug into the granite hillsides to follow the promising veins. Hard rock mining demanded skills, treatment facilities, and finances that most prospectors and early day miners did not possess.

It seemed to become a never-ending struggle to raise the funds to develop the properties. And, somehow they had to have a smelter built, where the ore could be crushed and, by some process, the gold, and perhaps silver, would be separated from the unprofitable gangue, or waste rock. Until this all could be accomplished, mining would languish.

That, in the eyes of the hopeful, remained all that was needed to turn Ouray into another Comstock or gold-rush-era California. But what had Ben Franklin observed about living on hope and dying of starvation?

The editor of the *Times* understood this need for support and hoped for a better reality to come quickly. In the June 16, 1877 paper, he bluntly addressed the problem, "Ouray is no exception to other new mining camps." Its future prosperity "depends upon works for reduction of the ore." Plenty of talk and plans echoed around the town and surrounding mountains, but, as yet, no construction project had started. Another problem needed to be resolved. What process would successfully and profitably work on Ouray's ores?

By that fall, a smelter had been built and rebuilt, because the initial process had not successfully worked, a not unusual occurrence in a new mining district. "Ore is coming in in gratifying quantities," the paper observed in its September 21 issue. However, coming winter weather was already threatening to curtail mining operations and shipping ore.

A year later (September 14, 1878), the paper reported that several reduction works had operated off and on during the past year. Then, it sadly observed – it "is regretted that more satisfactory results have not been reached." Finally, the article concluded with a lament that echoed familiarly throughout the mining West – "We live in hopes that the mines and [milling and smelting] machinery all will be in order for the early season of 1879."

In one of the first issues of the *Solid Muldoon*, October 10, 1879, the familiar cry was heard again, "Ouray needs reduction and smelting works." The writer went on to say, "We have a camp capable of producing hundreds of tons of ore per day, but [not] a home market for a pound of it worth anything near its real value."

The result of two years' of mining production, 1878-79, in Ouray County, slightly topped $109, 000, mostly in silver. That amount paled in comparison to Colorado's silver bonanza of the day, Leadville. It soared over $13, 000,000 in the same period. This, then, was the environment in which Dave Day and his press prepared to publish a new newspaper. His chosen community held high hopes and bubbled over with youthful enthusiasm. Assuredly, Ourayites believed, a promising future awaited them, if all went well.

Day was getting in on the ground floor, and, for a young man just starting a new career, the West symbolized a place to put down roots. Had not America's most famous newspaperman, Horace Greeley, written, "If you have no family or friends to aid you, and no prospect opened to you there (where you live), turn your face to the great West, and there build up a home and fortune."

Even better known, was the phrase he used in an editorial, "Go West, young man, and grow up with the country," but he gave credit to John Soule, who had written it in an 1851 article. David F. Day was doing just that as he, and his newspaper, elbowed their way into Ouray's present and future.

CHAPTER 4

Welcome to Ouray

hen Dave Day and his newspaper made their debut on September 5, 1879, Ouray already had given birth to two other papers. The *San Juan Sentinel* had come and gone, but the *Ouray Times* remained alive, gutsy, and feisty. It would be the *Muldoon*'s thorn-in-the-side local rival until its demise in June of 1886.

While it was not unusual to have more than one newspaper in a mining community, there often proved little enough advertising, or readers, for one to survive. Like so many other businesses, editors hoped to make a start in a new, "booming" camp and grow with it as it evolved into a town as its supporting mines gained prosperity and fame.

In San Juan country, from 1879 to 1885, the newspaper business was a chancy proposition at best. By 1879, four newspapers had been published in Silverton, but only one remained. Hinsdale also saw four with one left standing; and, in new Durango, nine had come and seven gone. Nor was this solely a San Juan phenomenon.

Leadville boomed and prospered at the same time. While much larger, richer, and nationally better known, the same pattern emerged. It had given birth to an astounding twenty-one newspapers between 1878-85. Of those, only four remained on the newsstands by the spring of 1885.

For whatever reason, Ouray had beaten the odds with two out of three surviving. However, no love was lost between the *Times* and *Muldoon*, as they fought like cats and dogs for readers and advertisers. It started when the *Times* welcomed Day and his paper, and opened with both editorial barrels firing.

After many tribulations and trials the Solid Muldoon *has made its appearance. In selecting this as its field of operations we believe it has made a mistake. There is not business here for two papers, and it is only a question of endurance which will hold the field. We accept the issue, and propose to remain in the field. September 13, 1879*

The idea of Muldoon *concerning a tramway from the Mineral Farm [mine] to the N&O Smelter is about as fossilized and ancient as the original Muldoon. The plan was discussed four months ago, but decided to be impracticable and given up. Will the* Muldoon *next tell us that carbonates have been struck in Leadville? September 13, 1879*

The Times *is under lasting obligations to the* Muldoon *for its thoughtfulness in issuing on Friday and that we might gather news items from it. The great difficulty is to tell what is news from what is gas; the latter largely predominating. September 20, 1879*

We wish to tell the Muldoon *a story in our youthful days. We once mistook a polecat for a pretty little kitten and proceeded to pet it a little. The scent of the rose hangs round that suit of clothes yet. Likewise, we first mistook the editor of the* Muldoon *for a gentleman, and—but the application is easy. October 4, 1879*

Last Sunday, a letter was received here from Mr. Geo. Sherman, agents clerk at Los Pinos, containing some information in regard to the Utes, directed to 'ed's Times *and* Muldoon. *The* Muldoon *editor happened to be present at the time and with commendable enterprise seized the letter, and with commendable enterprise issued an extra next morning as a special to the* Muldoon, *not even having the courtesy to inform this paper of the fact of the receipt of the letter. No comment on these facts is necessary. October 12, 1879*

The Ute issue involved the killing of their agent Nathan Meeker; and the cry resounded to remove them somewhere, anywhere, away from Ouray and out of Colorado. This topic will be discussed in a later chapter.

Meanwhile, the *Muldoon's* first issue carried a long "Salutatory," telling its readers what the paper planned to accomplish, what its editorial policy would be, and where it was going to position itself in the world of 19th century journalism. This was done in a lengthy editorial that stretched from one column into the top of another and included some epic sentences.

The undersigned have commenced the publication of a weekly newspaper at Ouray, to be known as THE SOLID MULDOON, *which in both matter and style they hope to render acceptable to the entire community.*

The great aridity for news has become one of the distinguishing characteristics of modern life, and the source that gratifies this with the least delay, the clearest conciseness and most unquestioned veracity, can not fail of commending itself to intelligent people everywhere, or of holding a front rank against all competition; and the current events of the week, at home and abroad, collected without regard to trouble or expense, and promptly presented to our readers will be one of the leading features of the paper, rendering its influence more widely effective and utilizing its energies to the utmost possible advantage.

It will therefore be the purpose to secure fullness and accuracy of news reports, and to have the criticisms on current events marked by fairness and candor; and believing the truth to be the highest obligation which a newspaper owes to its readers, they shall at all times publish the essential facts relating to public affairs, reserving the privilege of commenting upon them as they are related to right and wrong.

The chief commanding feature of THE SOLID MULDOON will be its devotion to the interests of the great mining region of the West—the San Juan Country—and especially of the people of the town and county of Ouray, to the furtherance of which, by the encouragement of public and private enterprise, the untiring energies of the whole management will be directed.

It will be the object of THE SOLID MULDOON in a political sense to sustain the principles of the Democratic party, especially in their practical relation to the growth, prosperity and legitimate rights of the Great West; to advocate such measures as will most effectually tend to relieve this section from the evils that have been thrust upon it by class legislation and a centralized money power; to defend the right of local self government, and in all proper ways to bring about such reforms and changes of policy as the public good requires. In assuming this position it will be the endeavor of the paper to pursue a fearless, square, independent of all party dictation, only so far as it may represent an organized effort in behalf of any just cause. To be a paper of the party, but not of the mere politician; to be a paper of the people, but not of rings, cliques or schemes that seek in any way to betray the popular confidence, will be its aim.

While maintaining views upon Local, State, and National questions which may be at variance with those of a portion of the community, we cheerfully grant the right of free discussion to those of opposing views, and at the same time extend the use of our columns for all legitimate purposes connected *with the publication of such a journal. As it will be our great ambition to publish a paper whose presence will be always welcome, with an influence always good in the home circle, we do not hesitate to appeal to the mothers, wives and daughters who give to that circle every hope it has of heaven, to lend us not only their smiles, but their cordial efforts. The proprietors have entered upon a journalistic venture in the firm belief that the wants of an enterprising community like this demand it; that another paper vigorous in its management, positive in it views, and thoroughly alive to the interests of the people whose patronage it hopes to win will be crowned with speedy and abundant success. Having such a faith, and being resolute to show it by our works, we present* THE SOLID MULDOON *to the candid criticism of the public, confidently relying upon a measure of patronage corresponding with the merits of the undertaking, and promising to devote a lifetime to insure it success.*

All these words proved more than just editorial "blurb," David Day would stand by them throughout his journalistic career. There were those, however, among his critics who did not think the paper's influence was "always good in the home circle," despite what the *Muldoon* proclaimed.

In the following years, Day always made a point of commemorating the paper's founding anniversary with an editorial. They became very much shorter as the years went by as will be shown by the following two examples, 1881 and 1884.

Two years ago the MULDOON *was turned loose upon the community under the auspices that were anything but favorable—launched upon the 'sea of journalism.' In the face of a severe San Juan winter, and with an indebtedness that would have disheartened a Methodist congregation. The*

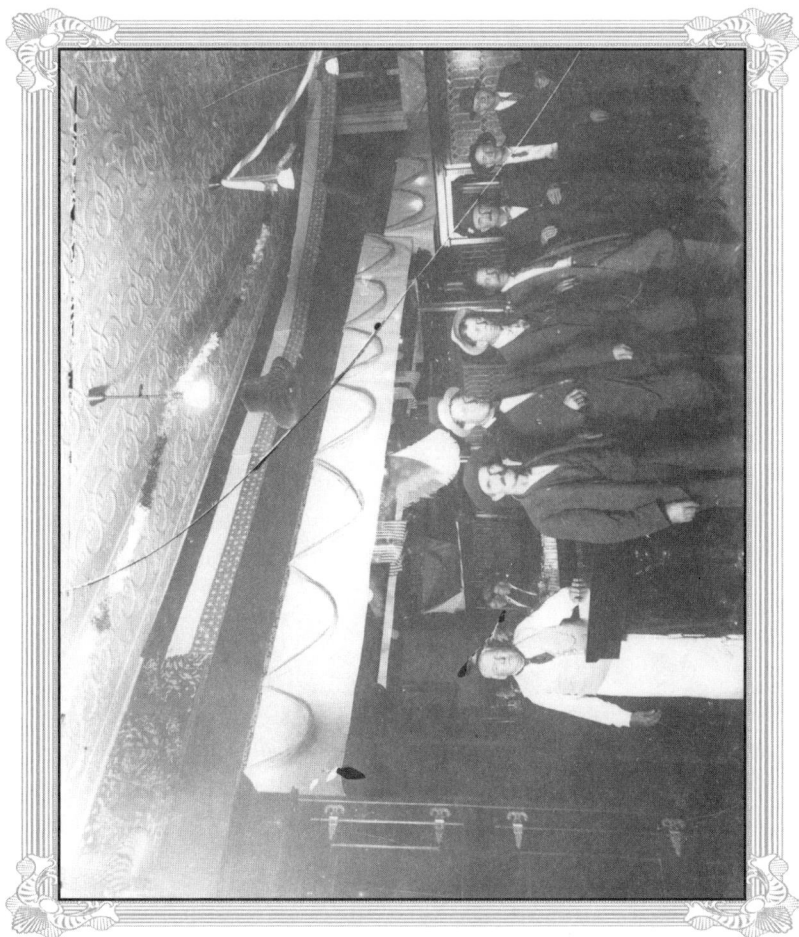

Unidentified Ouray saloon in the 1890s. Ruth and Marvin Gregory Collection

obstacles that we have surmounted have been numerous and vexatious, and can only be realized by those who have experienced the delightful occupation of engineering a red hot weekly two hundred and twenty-five miles from railroad faculties.

To-day, through the liberal patronage of a generous and warm-hearted people, we emerge from the brush in an enlarged form and with the largest subscription list of any publication in San Juan.

The future as in the past, we shall denounce and expose every mining corporation that we know to be a fraud, as well as those who seek, by misrepresentation to palm their worthless stock upon an unsuspecting public. Will devote our energies towards advancing the interests of Ouray county and her people. Look after the oppressed, care for the widows, worship in accordance with and vote the democratic ticket without declaration, [unable to read] amalgamation, erasure or scratch.

With this issue we enter upon our fifth volume without a struggle. We feel a delicacy in making any future promises for the Lord only knows what a Day may bring forth. However, we feel constrained (guess that's the correct word) to announce the politics and religion of the MULDOON will remain unchanged. So long.

On August 18, 1882, the paper announced. "The *Solid Muldoon* was sold to-day to D. F. Day purchasing all the property at a small advance on the original cost. Changes, if any, will be announced in the next issue." Day, previously listed as manager, now had sole control of his paper. It proved more than he could handle, financially or otherwise, and by December, he sought a partner.

Owing to increase of business, which necessarily multiples the cares of any newspaper office, and finding unsatisfactory to have details of importance to journalism success entirely in the hands of salaried help, we have decided to offer for sale an undivided one half interest in the Solid Muldoon.*"*

Not one to downplay his paper, he continued. "The *Muldoon* is the best piece of newspaper property in Southwestern Colorado, has the largest circulation of any publications in this section of the state, and is published in the best camp in the San Juan."

Without question, David Day enjoyed himself. He wrote in the January 27, 1882 edition:

The Muldoon *is two years and five months old and it is indeed a source of pleasure to look back over that period and be able to say without fear of contradiction that we have never missed an issue or suffered ourself to be asked twice to take a drink—punctuality is our boss grip.*

Being a "modest" chap, Day, in the October 4, 1879 issue, published comments which appeared in other newspapers about the new *Muldoon*. This not unusual custom provided a tip of the hat before the editorial whacking started.

The Muldoon *sticks to the mind, indelible and fixed, like a plaster to a poor man's ribs.* Dolores News

The Solid Muldoon *is the queer title of a rattling new paper just started in Ouray. If it keeps up its lick as it starts in, it will be popular in the San Juan.* Georgetown Miner

It starts out on Solid Muldoon *basis, a real representative of the rich region it represents.* Denver Times

One of its editors was, we believe, who first wittily dubbed his fellow citizens Ouraying Outangs. He has shown quite as much originality in naming his paper. Silver World

Ably editor, well printed and 'solid' for the democrats. Pueblo Democrat

Nor did Day stop there, every so often in his paper he quoted another comment about that "wonder," the *Solid Muldoon.*

The Omaha Herald *pronounces the Muldoon the brightest paper in Colorado. There's taste for yea.* Omaha Herald, *1881*

But for Dave Day's brains the SOLID MULDOON *would never be heard of outside Ouray County. He is very much a bigger man than the paper and it can't get along without him.* Denver Tribune, *July 21, 1881*

Ouray has an uncompromising advocate and defender in the Muldoon. *Dave Day deserves a crown of glory for what he has done, and is doing for Silvery San Juan.* Fort Collins Courier, *1884*

CHAPTER 5

Urban
Rivals

In the ruthless, heartless world of 19th century urbanization, it proved not only crucial for a community to have a newspaper to proclaim its virtues and defend its honor, but to have an outspoken, unfettered, and quotable advocate. The mining camp, or town, without one was lost indeed. Dave Day and his *Solid Muldoon* matched these expectations perfectly. Ouray, the San Juans, and even Colorado benefited from his newspaper and his readers must have enjoyed themselves.

His chief protagonists, those rival communities in and around the San Juans, caught most of his "barbs." Nonetheless, Day was not adverse to tackling those newspapers and communities beyond. None escaped his ever-alert eye and prickly pen. Dave could skewer them in a few short words.

The small mining hamlet of Animas Forks hardly received a mention. It posed no threat to Ouray.

> *Animas Forks is to have a newspaper called the* Pioneer. *Animas Forks in addition to a saloon and hitching post, has several un-patented 'mother veins' and twelve dogs. May 5, 1882.*

Lake City lay almost directly east of Ouray, but a mountain barrier stood in the way. Nonetheless, the town had been one of the early "gateways" to the region. Two 12,000 foot passes—Engineer and Cinnamon—were located west of the community and brought travelers into the heart of the mountains.

> *We don't like to cast discredit on Lake City for we admire it very much as a place of resort for invalids, but it is certainly*

too far from Ouray to ever make much of a town. October 24, 1879

Much of the rudeness and lack of refinement in Lake City may be traced to the frequent delays in the mails from Ouray. March 12, 1880

Lake City has never produced any philosophers, prize fighters or statesmen, but when it comes to starving out preachers, she holds the age. April 16, 1880

Lake City are just a little too far from Ouray to ever amount to much. October 14, 1881

A wagon load of delicacies was brought over from Lake City last week. The owner said that half buried village had no need of delicacies, bacon and Taos lighting being the universal bill of fare. February 4, 1881

The Red Mountain Mining District, between Silverton and Ouray, boomed briefly in the 1880s. It became a major bone of contention between the two towns, both claiming the district as theirs.

Red Mountain City, San Juan county, is a magnificent ruin; the entire city—consisting of one roofless log cabin and a dilapidated tent—is buried in the snow. We venture the prediction that in less than one year from to-day all traces of that once flourishing (?) town will disappear from the face of the earth. Kase why. Too far from the Red Mountain mines. February 9, 1883

Red Mountain City (?) is located at an altitude of 10,894 feet, according to the bench stakes on the D. & R. G. survey, while

*Red Mountain proper is a neat, cozy camp, and conveniently
located in the midst of the mines. Red Mountain City (?) is
simply a cheap advertising fraud, gotten up to gull prospectors into entering the Red Mountain district via Silverton.
The railroad fare to Silverton alone is double the passenger
tariff to Ouray, and you are twenty-four hours longer in
route. March 9, 1883*

While gold and silver had been discovered in the Rico area as
early as 1869, the camp had been a "Johnny come lately." Located
on the isolated western edge of the San Juan mining district, the
town of Rico did not emerge until 1878. Like many mining districts
and camps, its fortunes rose and fell, and isolation plagued it until
the railroad finally arrived in 1891. None of this put Rico beyond
Day's notice.

*The Rico Cemetery has been staked as a placer claim. Even a
graveyard is not safe in the sinful camp. October 10, 1879*

*If Rico expects to get up a reputation as a booming carbon-
ate camp, she must begin to do some shooting—plain knock
downs don't go. April 23, 1879*

*A Rico Preacher delayed services ten minutes in order to give
the Deacon an opportunity to sell pools in a dog fight. It is
evident humanity holds a tender place in the Christian heart.
April 16, 1880*

*Rico wants a hospital. A burro-pital is plenty good enough for
that wicked village. May 7, 1880*

*. . . Now the great trouble with Rico has been 'exaggeration.'
We say, and say it in a spirit of kindness, that the Dolores*

News has erred in advertising Rico as the best 'carbonate camp in the world.' Such fabulous 'ads' are calculated to encourage a class of immigration that is of no particular benefit to Rico or any other camp. We have had a much better opportunity judging the effect than the News has. During the past ten days scores of individuals have invaded our sanctum seemingly for no other purpose than cussing Rico. A careful inquiry into their troubles disclosed the fact that somebody charged them a whole dollar for a meal, [the] camp don't begin to come up to Leadville; best mines all staked; dance houses stocked with homely virgins; twenty-five cents for the meanest kind of whiskey and other equally injurious faults. July 2, 1880

Silverton, just across the mountains, south of Ouray, became a special Day target. In many ways it emerged as Ouray's chief rival; and when the Denver & Rio Grande Railroad reached there in 1882, that fact further infuriated "railroadless" Ouray and its editor. Jealousy reared its head repeatedly. Day saw little good or redemption in this "Sodom and Gomorrah."

People over at Silverton are beginning to punch the saw-dust out of the cracks and crawl out from under the stoves. This is a sure sign of spring. March 12, 1880

Silverton is a delightful village—Silverton is—certainly it is—Silverton is pleasantly located and surrounded by a continuous chain of rich and paying mines; the people there are generous , hospitable and Democratic; the village has a population of two hundred thousand, one hundred and ninety eight thousand eleven hundred and eight of whom are selling bug juice while the remainder are engaging raising bananas, paper cambric and other tropical vegetables. Silverton, in

*addition to John R Curry [rival editor] has several station-
ary saloons and a church—the church was a financial venture but the management feel certain of renting it for a dance
house in the spring. The agricultural outlook in Silverton is
very discouraging the heavy expense connected with putting
Westinghouse air brakes on the plows and rough locks on
the mules coupled with the unavoidable necessity of irriga-
tion with a horse syringe renders agriculture up hill work.
September 24, 1880*

*Over at Silverton when the semi-monthly mail arrives it has
to be dumped down through the chimney of the post office.
The snow is 25 feet deep and the air holes can only be kept
open by the exercise of eternal vigilance. February 19, 1880*

*Silverton is now referred to as 'the bride of the north pole.'
January 14. 1881*

*Silverton's population is increasing. But then Silverton's crop
of hoodlums invariably doubles up about cucumber time.
August 12, 1881*

*If Silverton had a little warmer climate and a little better
brand of whiskey, almost any person could be content to live
there who hadn't lived in a live town like Ouray. February
4, 1881*

*Twenty-six plain drunks, twelve dog fights, nine horse races,
two pistol matinees and one bit-his-ear-off at Silverton on
the fourth. Silverton is losing her grip. The old-timers are
not taking the same interest in the nation's holiday that once
characterized them. July 15, 1881*

We expect the Silverton papers to keep up appearances, as they have done since the camp started—by repeated and inconsistent lying—but when it comes to an outsider, who is indebted to Ouray and her citizens for board and medical treatment for months, it is just one step beyond the limits of common decency and dog gratitude. January 26, 1883

Silverton has huge drifts of snow piled around every house, and yet she is not happy. February 2, 1883

Silvertonites are tying to sell their smelter to the Chinese residents of that village for a Joss House. March 2, 1883

There is no smallpox in Silverton. Smallpox never tackles a corpse. March 16, 1883

She [Silverton] may, in the course of a number of years, make a fifth-class mining camp; but until she does her production will never amount to anything but blasted hopes, snow-shoe rabbits and very poor charcoal. February 2, 1883

Silvertonites are sitting on the chimney tops of their snowed under cabins bragging about their advantages as a spring resort. Over in Silverton they have 11 months winter and four week late—damlate spring. March 2, 1883

Silverton has a heart. We saw it going in, a few days since—three gamblers, two women and a 'yeller dog.' April 27, 1883

It costs Silverton two hundred and forty-eight dollars per month for a small pox nurse. Ouray hit the bull's eye when she quarantined angst that village. We have an eye to business over on this side of the hill. May 25, 1883

They had a regular parrot and monkey time over in the char-coal country last week. The 'tin-horns' captured Silverton, high water washed Chattanooga two miles further down the creek, cyclone blew Congress town up against the Hinsdale county line, and John Curry changed shirts. June 15, 1883

Silverton has one decided advantage over Ouray. They have ice the year around and it don't cost a cent; here it is two cents per pound. June 22, 1883

Silverton indulged in a parade and fireworks last week. Actuating motive—'nother car of ore from San Miguel, and two loaded jacks from Picayanne gulch. Wonderful village, that Silverton. August 10, 1883

Hello, Silverton! Have you heard from Red Mountain? The Ouray side of it? Recent discoveries in the National Belle and Guadalupe have placed corner lots in Silverton on a par with Confederate bonds. July 13, 1883

During the recent cold snap a Silverton man was frozen out of a game of centante with a cold deck. Terrible climate they have over the hill. February 8, 1884

Drummers say it is so dull and quiet over in Silverton that you can hear a gumdrop. Isn't actually enough of the energy in the artic village to get up a scandal. Mercy, mercy, what a horrid place Silverton must be. August 29, 1884

Now that sleighing is good let us all go over and raid Silverton. December 12, 1884

Silverton is blessed with two feet of snow, while Ouray has enough to lay the dust. PS. It required about eighteen inches to settle the dust in the Magnolia Metropolis. December 12, 1884

The hills around Silverton are strewn with frozen ground-hogs. When a ground-hog deliberately walks out and allows the elements to congeal his carcass, it is a terrible bad case of disgust and one that speak volumes in favor of the Magnolia route. March 28, 1884

Silverton merchants advertising bargains in heating stoves, while Ouray venders are putting on parasols and summer goods. The Almighty, in drifting for spring, seems to have used Silverton for a dump. May 23, 1884

Gathering wild flowers is the popular caper for the belles and beaux, and the mountain sides are fragrant and radiate with them. Poor Silverton, the snow has not disappeared sufficiently to allow the empty bean cans to show up, but if the weather continues warm they will have flowers late in August. May 16, 1884

Silverton is agitating a 4th of July blow-out. Snow-shoe races, rowing matches, coasting and a polar bear hunt will perhaps be the principal attractions.
May 30, 1884

Several Ourayites will go to Silverton on the 4th of July to witness the coasting and snowshoe races. June 13, 1884

The average Silverton woman never appears half so attractive as when masked [discussing masked ball]. *The majority of them are so dumpy they have to stand on a chair to scratch their backs, and the remainder are so lofty that the average masker would have to hook his toes in the kilt of their basques to get a good bite. It is in Ouray, you find symmetry in human architecture. September 9. 1884*

Silverton has already enjoyed a snow slide. Silverton's luck is simply immense. October 31, 1884

Isolated San Miguel/Telluride, southwest of Ouray, caught Day's attention occasionally.

Telluride is camp just a booming, capitalists and hoodlums every description and nationality pouring in. July 1, 1881.

[Then Dave visited the new camp and actually praised it]

This camp is decidedly the largest and most prosperous in the [San Miguel] valley. They have a decided advantage over their more pretentious rivals, Miguel City and Pandora, in point of location and natural advantages and embraced within their population, a sufficient number of interesting ladies to make life agreeable and rob solitude of all its charms. July 29, 1881

Day soon changed his mind about rival Telluride:

Telluride has seven lawyers and two dance halls, 0 churches, 000 school houses. Mercy, what a wicked village. August 16, 1883

Durango, the child of the D&RG, might lie across three 10,000 foot mountain passes from Ouray, but that did not stop Day. The rivalry became all the more animated when Durango gained that nineteenth century wonder, the railroad. Meanwhile, the railroad completely bypassed its older neighbor Animas City on the way into the mountains. Animas City was doomed, such was the iron horse's significance.

Durango went through a rough period of nine months after its September 1880 birth. That lasted until a city government was organized in May and June of 1881. Not one to miss a chance, Day never failed to point such things out.

Durango has reaped the ordinance closing her dance houses. The sudden prostration of her leading industry hurts. September 30, 1881

Durango is losing her grip. For the six months ending August 1, they only had seventeen divorces, against thirty-two for a corresponding period last year. But then the last session of the Methodist conference was held in Leadville. August 19, 1881

Durango would be a good place for an obelisk. It's the land of Faro. April 15, 1881

Parties attending Easter services at Durango are requested to leave their six-shooters with the janitor, who will return the same at the close of exercises. April 1, 1881

Durango wouldn't make a respectable flag station on the Salt Lake extension. In addition to being on the wrong side of the divide, Durango is too far from Gunnison to ever amount to anything. June 22, 1882

Durango has seen her palmist days. Two years ago was the time to have unloaded lots and real estate in that agricultural precinct. June 22, 1883

Durango's permanent exhibit of San Juan ores has been packed away in a box until spring. The constituency did not bite. November 23, 1883

Durango is howling for an annual term of U. S. Court. Del Norte is about as near a graveyard as judge Hallet cares to get. The idea of torturing litigants by compelling them to visit Durango, Perfectly awful. September 21, 1883

Durango's gold excitement was only of short duration. Deceased's wife came to the front and made affidavit that at the time of burial her husband's teeth were filed with zinc. September 21, 1883

Half of Durango's and two-thirds of Silverton's population are up in Red Mountain dodging the small pox. Durango and Silverton will soon loom up as two orphans. May 11. 1883

The Durango Southwest speaks of that dog-fennel [a "strong smelling weed"] village as a metropolis. If Durango is metropolis, what's Saguache? May 11, 1883

Durango sheets have the gall to spout about smelters and wholesale advantages, when the facts are well, look at the bullion statistics of Colorado and see just what a fly-speck La Plata county is. A hay-baler and potato-hook is about what Durango needs. May 25, 1883

In Durango the snow is so deep and the women so short that the latter have to climb out of the sky-lights and stand on the chimney top to scratch their backs. February 22, 1884

The habit of the Durango people had fallen into that of using ten cent mustard plaster for undershirts—rendered the suffering greater during the recent Artic blizzard than it would have been had not the supply of gunny sacks been exhausted in relieving Silverton. February 22, 1884

A drove of eighty-five reindeer passed through Ouray, yesterday, en route to Durango, Silverton and other points in the polar regions. Feb. 29, 1884

Silverton's representative men are welcome to locate in Ouray, but the gaar-gat and bobtail elements will find Durango a more congenial field. We have a tramp ordinance over here. March 7, 1884

Durango sheets assert that there is not much doing in the matrimonial line in their hamlet. The preference of the opposite sex for something more substantial than gamblers, burglars and veteran bums seems to increase with commendable rapidity on the Wingate trail. March 9, 1884

The wall street panic will not effect Durango. In fact, the news will scarcely reach that village before October. May 23, 1884

Ouray will be a populous and prosperous mining camp when Durango is a forgotten fraud. May 30, 1884

Occasionally Day ventured further afield to let loose a blast. Denver provided a favorite target, which will be discussed in more detail in a later chapter, but so did other communities.

Pueblo has actually had a first class wedding. The press throughout the state should notice this event as it is the only important local occurrence since the railroad war last June. April 23, 1880

Pueblo's efforts to secure the capitol has, to say the least, effected a radical change in the conduct of a portion of her people. They now wait until the tourist reaches his hotel before robbing him. August 5, 1881

Which is the most destructive to human life, Denver's building inspector, or her opium joints. April 8, 1881

The Rocky Mountain News, *a paper published in Denver, characterizes the press of that city as the 'press of the State,' all of which is exceeding rough on the patent insides. March 25, 1881*

Nearby and, thus, one more Ouray rival—Montrose also became a favorite Day whipping "boy."

The owls and buzzards are negotiating for winter quarters in Montrose. It certainly will be secluded and quiet enough. September 15, 1882

Montrose will never amount to even a dog-fennel town. November 17, 1882

Montrose is the most forsaken, desolate, barren looking hole in all Colorado. It is located in the midst of a vast alkali bed where greasewood and sage brush refuse to grow. November 24, 1882

Montrose is a little dull at the moment only thirteen saloons running. August 18, 1882

The Montrose Messenger *advertises that Alkali patch, as an 'agricultural center.' Of all the barren spots on earth*

Montrose takes the lead. It equals in point of attraction the staked plains. December 22, 1882

The alkali dust at Montrose varies in depth from six inches to nine feet. And yet those people want to sell lots to strangers. December 15, 1882

The Red Mountain boom has about depopulated Montrose. Very few are left and those remaining are too badly alkalized to travel. April 13, 1883

Just so long as Montrose continues to harbor tin-horns, pimps and other species of human nuisances, just so long will Montrose continue to find the murdered bodies of her citizens in the rivers and by-ways in and around that village. Ouray has fired them and they will stay fired. August 22, 1884

Montrose did not suffer alone. Day took no prisoners when it came to nearby urban rivals and other Colorado towns.

The Loveland Reporter *devotes two columns per week to 'Bible lessons.' The law against carrying concealed weapons must been in force in that vicinity. April 21, 1882*

The third correction line gives Delta about seven miles of the Uncompahgre Valley. Another survey will give Montrose the cold sweats and leave her with nothing more conducive to prosperity and taxable property than the Messenger *and Andy Woodruff's wardrobe. August 31, 1883*

Gunnison to have street cars. A wind-break is about what Gunnison needs. April 27, 1883

Dave Day about the time he left Ouray and went to Durango
DG Collection, Denver Public Library, OCHS Collection

The Grand Junction News *calls our attention to the fact that another 'brick building has gone up.' A village located one hundred miles from timber could scarcely go back on brick. February 15, 1884*

Gunnison's inducement to capitalists, outside of a 20x40 delinquent list and an indebtedness almost equal to the total valuation of the county, are purely imaginary. Gunnison should indulge in precipitation. December 12, 1884

A prominent citizen of Gunnison has just died in an Aspen dance house. Something peculiar about those Gunnison folks. They will stay in that hole until death is inevitable, and then pull out and get into better society before passing away. February 27, 1885

The Del Norte Prospector *complains of lack of religious service in that village. Wonder if it ever occurred to the* Prospector *man that the average Del Norte soul was not worth saving. December 12, 1884*

Our mining friends in the east who desire to invest in town lots should examine the many advantages offered by Grand Junction a cross-road abortion on the D. & R. G.'s Utah extension. They have less than three thousand acres of patented land in the county, twelve hundred and eighty of which is carved up in 'town lots,' and offered to a suffering public at prices ranging from three to five hundred dollars per lot. There's gall for you. January 1, 1884

GRAND JUNCTION Queen Fraud of the Sunset Slope . . . An Empire Founded on Greed, Gall and Prevarication [Article headline]. January 11, 1884

We desire to call the attention of our readers on the outside to the fact that Grand Junction, the 'Queen of the Sunset Slope' had 3,300 town lots for sale and the county casts 704 votes. January 18, 1884

This season we fully expect 200 valentines from Grand Junction, and a like number from other jim-crow hamlets. February 8, 1884

The Grand Junction Democrat (?) failing to find any statistic refuting the charge against the village as a town-site fraud, launches out in a vein of falsehood and abuse that curs and cowards use at long range, couch their pet phrases in language that emanates only from an intellectual diseased and addled by the long and continued practice of onanism [ornerism]. It is indeed very mortifying to be brought into contact with such disgusting and degrading emblems of self-pollution, but here in the West distance sometimes compels gentlemen to endure for a season the rot and cowardly production of such puppets. February 1, 1884.

Grand Junction is unquestionably the greatest town lot fraud ever inaugurated. Lots on the summit of the divide are just as valuable, and a great deal cheaper. March 14, 1884

The delinquent tax list gave the 'Queen of the Sunset Slope' dead away. Nine hundred and fifteen town lots returned delinquent and on an average valuation of FIFTEEN DOLLARS per lot. Grand Junction isn't a town lot fraud; o no, it's Silwatch [Saguache]. May 30, 1884

Saguache wants gas, water works, street cars and an opera house. It must have a dance house, keno game or some other sign of prosperity to warrant such extravagant aspirations. February 10, 1882

Salida wants the capitol. Salida should confine her wants to her need and petition for a soap factory or dust consumer, Salida should. August 19, 1881

CHAPTER 6

Ouray Pride

David Day and Ouray became synonymous within a few years of the *Muldoon's* birth. Very little of the community's goings-on and individuals escaped his all-seeing eye and ever alert journalistic pen. He praised, prodded, provoked, but never procrastinated when it came to writing something about his town and its residents and visitors.

People stood on both sides of the fence when it came to appreciation of the *Muldoon's* efforts, as its outspoken editor readily admitted. Like him, or damn him, Ourayites, and others, read his weekly jottings.

What follows offers a potpourri, a sampling, of Day's observations, suggestions, criticisms, and whatever else came up as he discussed the events, the people, the very hustle, bustle, and enterprise, and sometimes the lack thereof, in his hometown and among its neighbors. Day missed very little.

> *We are near enough to the stars to do without street lamps this winter, but some different plan for supplying the water might be an advantage—it is necessary. November 14, 1879*
>
> *Why can't Ouray make an improvement in her water works? This donkey and cart business would not be very efficient in case we were visited by the fire fiend. November 14, 1879*
>
> *We wish to state to parties intending to emigrate to Colorado that Ouray offers the following inducement: unequaled climate, mineral springs, good wages, splendid school, fine agricultural and grazing lands, mines that are world beaters, excellent society and no preachers. May 4, 1880*

Ouray is one of the most pleasant summer resorts in Colorado. Hot and cold springs, way up fishing and hunting, delightful drives, picaresque and a brass band that never makes a night hideous unless the trouble is paid for in advance. July 8, 1881

Ouray is on the tidal-wave, and on for good. The activity now observed on every side, and more especially in mining and building circles is unprecedented in the history of San Juan camps. February 16, 1883

Ouray is the Comstock of San Juan, the Robert E. Lee [famous Leadville mine] *of the western slope, the birthplace of the Solid Muldoon and the home of many who have lost their fortunes but not their manhood—and some who have lost both. July 6, 1883*

Visitors to Ouray pronounce it the cleanest and most pleasantly located camp in the state. And it is. June 9, 1882

A host of drummers have visited town within the last two weeks. And if their countenance is a telltale Ouray is not a bad place to light in. April 21, 1882

LOOK UPON US!
Ouray, the Banner County of the San Juan Country!
The camp of Ouray, since it has been a camp (and unlike our more pretentious consumers beyond the divide, we are not as yet a city), has possibly encountered and overcome a greater number of vexatious obstacles than any other village in all Colorado. January 4, 1884

Ouray is the center of the universe, and we hereby give notice that all other alleged centers are frauds and base imitations. May 2, 1884.

Ouray's Hot Springs now attracts visitors from all the neigh-boring camps and with a railroad our village will become a popular resort for tourists and health seekers. Poor Silverton. August 15, 1884

Mr. [James] MacCarthy, the 'Fritz Mac' of Rothacker's Opinion, came in from Silverton on the hurricane deck of a bronco yesterday afternoon, and expresses his willingness to make affidavit that Ouray can double discount the scenic efforts of Royal Gorge and Black Canyon combined. He pro-nounces the grandeur of our surrounding as beautiful beyond description. August 15, 1884

Four boy babies in Ouray since the lst, and several townships yet to hear from. Wonderful town, this Ouray. July 11, 1884

The hose boys are having four stuffed clubs prepared to sue over the heads of such of our citizens as insist upon forgetting to keep their mouths shut during the progress of a fire. The Company annually elects officers for the purpose of giving orders and conducting the exercises and they don't care to have outsiders infringe upon the duties of their foreman and his assistants. March 21, 1884

Quite a number of our citizens have fallen into the habit of 'sending outside' for various articles of merchandise, and it is not in any sense commendable. Our merchants carry about every article the trade demands, and sell at as close margins as legitimate business will permit of, and as they are largely instrumental in bearing the burdens of taxation, should at least be given preference over an Eastern competition that cares lit-tle or nothing for the welfare of our people or commonwealth. Let the 'spending out' exercise cease. August 29, 1884

Let the city 'dads' wade in and have the streets put in a passable condition. The streets of Ouray are a disgrace to the town. Why are they not kept in better condition? September 5, 1884

If gambling and other species of vice are harbingers of booms, Ouray will certainly enjoy a full grown one this summer. May 23, 1884

The dance house element are gradually becoming convinced that the founders and solid stand-bys of Ouray have some rights that must be respected but if they continue skeptical and insist upon opening and conducting dens of infamy in each and every section of the town and thus openly defying decency and morality, the Muldoon will certainly advocate the enforcement of the State law against prostitution. There are entirely too many wives, mothers and daughters in Ouray to allow the 'pimps and 'herders' to run it. Our City Council has shown a disposition to permit certain social evils to remain undisturbed just as long as the limits or ordinary decency are respected, but when depraved nature and portable sin attempts to dictate to an element that has stood by the town since its inception, we grow sufficiently belligerent to either exact a limited amount of respect or fire the evil entirely. July 19, 1884

If the whole population of Ouray is going to get married, what the thunder's the use of going to a warmer altitude this winter. September 25, 1884

The painful and tedious regularity with which the average Ouray husband ignores the protestations of the Muldoon and continues to loaf and loiter around the various gin dives and sin breeding establishments of the village, should, at least, prompt our resident ministers to counsel them during their sober moments, and entreat them if possible to abstain from practices that must eventually lead to domestic discord, penury, and want. Respect for those excellent ladies who have the misfortune to call them husband prevents a publication of names, but we will cheerfully furnish our ministers with a list of those whom we honesty believe are rapidly drifting beyond the hope of human entreaty, and redemption. January 11, 1884

We do hope the good people on the outside will not allow their anxiety for our safety [Meeker massacre problems] *to lead them to exaggeration—Ouray is safe—chuck full of brave men—and the* Muldoon. *October 10, 1879*

Every merchant, lawyer, abstract rooster, saloonist, druggist, assayist, hardware and newspapah man should be compelled to clean up his own front yard and reserve the poll tax for the back streets and alleys. April 23, 1880

The amount of profanity indulged in by the little boys of Ouray is actually shocking. Parents should either break them of the obnoxious habit or else break their necks. Our ministers should call attention of mothers to this growing evil. April 2, 1880

We don't see why the city council does not enforce the sidewalk ordinance on the east side of Third Street. Let the city dads attend to this matter. July 9, 1880

Our city dads should begin casting around for a street commissioner. The streets and alleys do not wear a very inviting appearance. May 7, 1880

Town of Ouray,
circa 1880
Ruth and Marvin
Gregory Collection

Feb. 22d, 1880 the birthday of the man who was 'first in war, first in peace and first in the hearts of his countrymen,' came on Sunday last. But in our town not a demonstrate of any character was made, yes, there was one man, who did remember the occasion, and observed it by hoisting the American flag; . . . and that man was a German American. How soon our children forget us, how transient the glory of this world. February 27, 1880

Among the professions not yet represented in Ouray is a photographer. A good artist should succeed here. January 23, 1880

Our School House fund is sufficient inducement for all to make a few sacrifices. It's a good cause. Just like church festivals and entertainments wants the assistance of everyone in town. Don't forget it. February 6, 1880

Let us have a school house. Educate your children, and if you have none of your own, assist to educate your neighbors and thereby promote the cause of good government and humanity generally. February 6, 1880

We don't want any smelters within the corporate limits of our town, but if necessary might move the town. February 20, 1880

Our churches should be well patronized and the miners' reading room scheme encouraged. December 10, 1880

The troubadours of Ouray were out Saturday night, and discoursed music so sweet the even limpid waters of the Uncompahgre stopped and listened. December 10, 1880

In a town of this size nothing should occur to cause a division in the social circles. We are glad to see a decried disposition tending towards harmony and good feelings. December 10, 1880

Two of Ouray's prominent young men have notified our school that upon the completion of the school building they will adorn it with a three hundred dollar bell. Such enterprise and liberality is rarely met with in the ranks of bachelors. June 18, 1880

The Methodist ice cream festival at the Dixon house, Wednesday evening was very liberally patronized. The patronage being far in excess of the cream. August 6, 1880

Ouray's water works cost $29,000 and Ouray is amply able to pay for them. We are the only village in the San Juan that conducts the exercise upon a strictly metropolitan basis. Oh, we're way up. October 27, 1881

Our little village sports about fifteen pianos, and an endless number of organs, melodeons, violins, guitars, and other instruments of lesser magnitude, besides a good silver band, and what's more there are few towns in the State that has anymore skillful musicians than our cliff-encircled burg. November 18, 1881

Our City Marshall cannot be too exacting in this street cleaning business. Let his renovation be thorough and complete. April 18, 1881

The Muldoon favors raising the saloon license to three hundred dollars per annum and allowing the Marshal seventy-five dollars per month. If our saloon keepers would insist upon an ordinance compelling them to pay their license yearly in advance they would protect themselves from all tent saloon and summer dives. The latter is a species of doggery that migrates from camp to camp during the summer months, and sells at a reduced price a quality of whiskey that would paralyze a Ute. March 18, 1881

We would suggest to our efficient town marshal and police justice the propriety of studying the statutes and ordinances made there under, and of endeavoring to ascertain what the objects and purposes of the same are. The men selected for these positions are men possessed of judgment and discretion and they must not think that filling the town exchequer is making good officers or preserving the tone and dignity of the corporation. May 13, 1881

The town recorder is under indictment for larceny. Town Attorney Judge Judas Story under bonds for general meanness and one of the members of the city council selected as receiver(?). Oh Ouray is a bang up place. July 22, 1881

The only charge we visit upon the old [town] board is destitution of energy. They are too near the graveyard for western purposes. April 1, 1881

Hell has no fury like a town with two fusion tickets. April 1, 1881

The open ditches caused some of the freighters who visited town this week to use naughty words. October 21, 1881

The hose boys, in their first run of 100 yards, made coupling and threw water in thirty seconds. Good for scrubs. October 21, 1881

The fun-loving and hilarious portion of Ouray's people have in the past been exceedingly kind and generous to the Ouray string band but in the future, the band will either be compelled to secure a leader in place of Mr. Valentine or close up shop. 'Old Val' is growing just a little bit too infernal crank and mean for any one. July 8, 1881

The fire laddies did remarkably well at the Newhall fire. They saved the front gate, a large bucket of ice and the sawbuck. December 2, 1881

The public school is having a boom. Good teachers and everything in order is the cause of the large attendance. December 2, 1881

It would save quite a number of bruised shins if the obstructions on the sidewalks were removed. December 16, 1881

Ouray has more vitality than all the other towns in San Juan combined. Why, bless you, we pay eight dollar per gallon for ice cream, two bits a nip for tangleroot, fifty dollar for carrying concealed weapons, two hundred and fifty for a second handed town attorney, and are the only town in the state where a gentleman afflicted with kleptomania is eligible to the position of town recorder. Oh, yes, Ouray is a bang up place. June 24, 1881

In a few short weeks the 'gang' that have for years drawn their official salary with painful regularily, and feasted and fatted upon the tax-payer will step down and out. Their departure will be conspicuous for the absence of tears and other manifestations of sympathy. There will be no crape or other emblems of woe to herald their departure; no scalding weeps or violent outbursts of saddened grief will foretell the evacuation. November 23, 1883

This is the first season in the history of Ouray when the music of the hammer, saw, anvil and blast has been heard in February. We are free from snow and building is going ahead with a vigor that exhibits all the symptoms of a genuine boom. Our people merit all the prosperity that can be visited upon us. March 2, 1883

The city council in granting dance house licenses, should carefully consider the surroundings, and in all cases where the applicants seeks to open those dens of infamy in portions of the city frequented by the virtuous mothers and daughters of Ouray, licenses should be positively and emphatically refused. May 25, 1883

Rents are unnecessarily high in Ouray. We always make this discovery about the time the first of the month gets in sight. April 20, 1883

Our school house wears a kind of song and dance look. That red striping is simply abominable. December 21, 1883

This thing of enforcing the ordinance relating to prostitution and gaming on a few and allowing the many to escape is not justice. It is plain, unvarnished robbery. December 14, 1883

The reckless manner in which the soiled doves settle around in various portions of our once moral village should at least suggest a herd law. Let the evil be concentrated or bounced. February 16, 1883

This thing of putting in pipe, paying tax, and then having to carry water four blocks is not calculated to breed harmony. The council have our permission to resign in a body or separately. February 16, 1883

It is a sad commentary upon the morality and religious portion of our community, when an ex-pastor has to sell the church and lot upon which it stands in order to collect salary. First Presbyterian church sold [in] favor of George Smith. March 30, 1883

Every dollar expended by Ouray county in building roads will add hundreds to the taxable wealth of our county. Roads are necessity, county buildings are not. Let all this talk about court houses and jails be side-tracked until a good wagon road penetrates every camp in Ouray county. August 3, 1883

Eighty-five in the shade is not a very attractive advertisement for a summer resort; yet that is Ouray's average temperature for this week. June 29, 1883

The Salvation Army has struck Ouray at last and we are saved. July 6, 1883

Ouray is cursed with a gang who labor under the impression that they must be retained in office during their natural lives. They think the masses incompetent to choose their public servants, and never miss an opportunity to push themselves forward. They have no political creed that is permanent, and their interests in the advancement or welfare of any party depends solely upon their chances for office. The Muldoon is sick and sore of such presumptuous parasites, and trusts that the voters of both parties wills it down on them when the time arrives. June 22, 1883

Decoration day has passed, and not a flower of remembrance for our dear dead-gone-est, Thespian Club. June 1, 1883

The city council should by ordinance confine the social evil and dance-house elements to certain portions of the corporate limits. An ordinance preventing the opening of bawdy or dance-houses south of 8th Avenue, would meet the demands of decency, and give the scarlet portion of our community ample territory. May 11, 1883

There has never been a fire in Ouray, but then the Muldoon keeps the constituency sufficiently warmed up to justify a hose company. May 8, 1883

Let the wicked and ungodly read the 'Dance House' ordinance in this issue. May 18, 1883

Some naughty women have arrived in town the last few days. There must be a boom on the road in. April 14, 1882

The new council have extended to the editors of each of the publications an invitation to attend all meetings of the board. What! No more secret sessions. April 14, 1882

The blacksmiths in town, after their little round up on cut prices, have entered into an agreement to do work for an established price which will be printed and posted in their shops in open sight. April 28, 1882

We do not think there is a sensible man in the county who will oppose the voting of bonds for a court house. Our records demand a fire proof building and one in keeping with the taxable wealth of our county. August 11, 1882

Ouray is beginning to feel the want of a good string band. The music last night was a little thin and no mistake. December 1, 1882

False front buildings, Ouray, circa 1880-1885. Ruth and Marvin Gregory Collection

Ouray will need a spanker boom if the increase in kids continues. October 6, 1882

The town is over run with tin horn gamblers and sneak thieves. No less than a half dozen attempts at home breaking within the past week. It might not be sinful to insinuate that perhaps Ouray posses a secret organization that will make short work of the first victim. October 6, 1882

Ouray wants a shoemaker and wants one bad. August 25, 1882

The hose boys succeeded in throwing water nearly twenty-five feet over the flag pole last Tuesday. A great improvement on all former attempts. With such a force of water and such alert firemen Ouray property owners feel secure from the ravages of fire. July 21, 1882

Hold ups and attempted burglaries are getting thick. About time that this class of characters were weeded out of our garden, isn't it? July 21, 1882

The Muldoon favors a city council with sufficient intelligence to dispense with the employment of fourth rate legal talent. March 24, 1882

Only one death has occurred in town during the winter and that by accident. A good report on the health qualities of our climate. March 3, 1882

No school house; no court house; no jail; $20,000 in water works bonds; state, county, school, corporation, road, military and poll tax. There is certainly a pressed demand for a *city hall; also for a lunatic asylum.* [Editorial comment on question building town hall] *The* Muldoon *has always made it an object to advocate every needed improvement, but it strikes us that a town hall, in a village without either a schoolhouse or bridge accommodations for its people, is slightly superfluous. March 3, 1882*

The town hall business was inaugurated by a few cranks for the purpose of defeating the county commissioners in their efforts to arrange for county buildings. Before our city council are allowed to flirt with six or seven thousand dollars in town hall bonds there should be a search made for the twenty thousand just disposed of. March 10, 1882

The Muldoon *favors a straight democratic ticket and a board endowed with sufficient intelligence to disperse with the office of city attorney. March 10, 1882*

The opening ball given by the 'Bachelors Club' at the court house was a crowning success. The hall was handsomely decorated with the flags of our country, and the music as sublime and inspiring as has ever been heard, since the rocks and trees gave ear to Orpheus' lyre, or the children of Israel chanted the songs of Moses upon the banks of the Red Sea. The attendance was one of the largest and most fashionable ever assembled in Ouray, and the courtly quadrille, and knightly schottish and undulating waltz gave all who wish an opportunity to display their graces. The midnight lunch let additional energy to the occasion and the exercises were protracted until the dial hand indicated the hour of four. The boys were real naughty, but didn't we have a nice time. November 26, 1880

CHAPTER 7

Politics

A political animal, David Day prowled for a generation. Always a feisty, unrelenting, unrepentant Democrat, and "don't you forget it," he spared few victims. Being his usual maverick, curmudgeon self, he saw very little good in the Republican Party or its candidates—local, state, or national—or generally speaking its elected officials. That made him stand out in a state that in the 1870s into the late 1880s generally voted Republican.

Absolutely fearless, he praised and attacked, particularly during election years. Off years did not stop him either. He stood ready at all times to take up the Democratic banner and cause whether in personal or party criticism or praise for the "good guys." Partisan David took no political prisoners. Politics brought out the best and some believed the worst in the *Muldoon's* Day.

Briefly, during the 1882 campaign, he published a daily *Muldoon* to help his favorite candidates. "Our mission has been accomplished and the enterprise will be temporally abandoned until June when we trust the telegraphic facilities will enable us to continue permanently. Until then adieu." [November 10, 1882] Daily publication never resumed.

The outlying districts felt that Denver wielded too much power and received too many of political "loaves and fishes." The Western Slope, in particular, felt aggrieved. Realistically, however, the Western Slope was a newcomer politically compared to Colorado east of the Continental Divide. The region had little political influence or IOU's to collect and a limited number of experienced favorite sons to advance for office. None of that deterred Day for a moment, as he advocated his favorite candidates and party.

Any republican within the broad limits of Ouray County who would cast his vote for W. E. Beck the Atchison Topeka & Santa Fe candidate for supreme court judge, deserves to be disemboweled and throw out for buzzard bait. September 20, 1879

The Solid Muldoon *is the only Democratic journal in all the San Juan, but thank heaven our giant intellect enables us to come with the thieves and carpet baggers who run the machine organs. March 26, 1880*

The Muldoon *may have been guilty of many misdeeds, but there is no record on earth to show where we ever tried to 'bolt.' We go the straight unscratched Democratic ticket. October 14, 1881*

The campaign in San Juan promises to be both bitter and personal. The Muldoon *when not acting as an umpire will join in the round up. August 11, 1882*

Ouray democracy are in a splendid condition, harmony, brains and a determination to win. August 4, 1882

Repudiation is the mother-in-law of Republicans. December 4, 1881

Twenty years of Republican rule has brought polygamy to a state of perfecting rarely, if ever, attained by any other vegetable. February 18, 1881

The legislature convened in Denver on the fifth. There will be quite a number of statesmen developed in the next forty days. January 14, 1881

The Colorado legislature may have contained a number of blockheads, but certainly a sufficient number of dunderheads to adopt any local option of woman suffrage foolishness. February 18, 1881

The nomination of Gen. [Winfield Scott] Hancock [1880 Democratic presidential nominee] was a godsend to the American Republic, and never since the days of Washington has there a nomination ever come more manifestly from the hearts of the American people. July 2, 1880

The speeches at the Republican meeting last Tuesday night were disappointing. The speakers went over the beaten track threshing the old straw. They were down among the dead men all the time. The tariff and the famous Indian problem were ignored, while the air was laden with the old story of the flag with 37 stars, fulsome eulogies of the Republican party and blazed predictions of the coming election. August 27, 1880

Every Democrat will vote the straight ticket. Our national, state and county officers are representative men and defeat ain't in the pins. October 23, 1880

A vote for Hancock is a vote to bury sectional strife, a vote against Chinese immigration, a vote in favor of alleviating the burdens of the laboring masses and a vote against bonanza kings and centralization. October 29, 1880

Democrats! Beware of Fraudulent voters.
He who shirks from challenging an illegal vote is a coward.
Stand by the polls. October 29, 1880

Day never let up on criticizing Republicans and praising Democrats:

It is remarkable to note the number of Republican newspapers for sale throughout the land. Even the patient inside organs sniff the inevitable. June 15, 1883

No small amount of the prosperity that Colorado now enjoys is due to the fact that our legislature only gets biennial whacks at the state treasury. January 26, 1883

The Republican State Committee will meet April 10th to agree upon a price list and arrange such other details as will tend to make the approaching auction a success. March 21, 1884

Democracy is the only barrier between the silver dollar and demonetization. May 16, 1884

The Republican victory in November 1880, and Hancock's defeat, disgusted Dave Day, who promptly gave his readers his reaction in the November 5 *Muldoon*. He could not resist barbs about the all important "silver issue." Already Coloradans were racing to the barricades and the pulpits about the steadily declining price of its most important mineral which threatened its economic mining foundation. Colorado, as they all knew, ranked number one in the United States in gold and silver production by 1880.

Now Easterners, bankers, foreigners and a host of others "schemed" to undermine, in Coloradans eyes, silver and, therefore, Colorado. They watched as country after country turned to the gold standard, basing their monetary systems on gold rather than silver with its unstable price. Were not silver and gold both "God's money" and the money of the Bible? They thought so and turned to the Federal Government for help.

Uncle Sam responded, after a fight, by agreeing to purchase silver and coin it. That helped, but did not provide the whole answer.

Ahead lay the "issue," the "cause"—the demand for a guaranteed price for silver at 16 to 1, or a $1.25 price per ounce based on gold's standard of $20 per ounce. It would be the issue throughout the fateful 1896 election, when William Jennings Bryan and silver went down in defeat. Where one stood on that question meant political success or suicide in Ouray County, and Colorado.

All of the quotes that follow are from the *Solid Muldoon* of November 5, as Day recovered from another Republican presidential victory:

> *Tuesday night we retired to our virtuous couch full of joy and hope. Wednesday morning we got up—haven't had an attack of hope since.*

> *The laboring men of the North deserve the yoke of slavery— or at least those of them that voted for James A. Garfield.*

> *The day of honest elections in America is passed and the sooner this country merges into a monarchy the better we will be satisfied.*

> *Oh! Where are the friends of my youth? Gone Republican of course.*

> *The nation's purse beat the gallant Hancock.*

> *Mining property that was valued at $45,000 two weeks ago can be bought to-day for one-third of the amount. Under Garfield's administration silver will be too common for wagon tires.*

Horace Tabor made his wealth in 1878-79 booming Leadville, and, as many Colorado mining men did, entered politics. Elected Lieutenant Governor in 1878, he had his eye set on the state's leading political prize, a United States Senate seat. He was not alone in that ambition. In those days, the state legislature elected the senator—or rather the majority vote of the dominant party therein did—allowing for political shenanigans and bribery.

Of course, Tabor had a problem that upset Victorian America. He was a divorcee, and he had "dallied neither wisely nor well" with a younger woman.

Tabor for Governor! Well won't the Muldoon have a pic-nic. Two more bottles in the back parlor. December 16, 1881

Tabor's seat for 30 days in the United States Senate is said to have cost him $200,000. A big price for so short a whistle. February 9, 1883

Denver and Leadville papers think the state owes Tabor a 'debt of gratitude.' Denver and Leadville may owe Mr. Tabor a debt of that kind, but when it comes to the state at large we suggest the check be drawn in favor of either William J. Palmer, Gov. John Evans or William H. A. Loveland. April 14, 1882

The appointment of Tabor [senate seat] would have been a compliment to imbecility, an ignoration of the south and an insult to virtue while that of [Thomas] Bowen would have resulted in placing a powerful weapon in the hands of one of the most gifted and unscrupulous politicians in the state. April 14, 1882

The mere mention of such mushroom statesman as [William] Hamill or Tabor for senate is an insult in virtue, ability, honor, and decency. Tis simply a compliment to mediocrity and prostitution—nothing else. November 17, 1882

The appointment of [George] Chilcott over Tabor and Bowen is the most commendable official act that Gov. Frederick W. Pitkin has ever been guilty of. This thing of conferring the highest honor with the gift of an executive upon a monied prostitute or renege politician is a base and infamous outrage upon honor, decency and virtue. What is Tabor? Let those who have been so conspicuous in advocating his claims in the senatorship go down in the hidden recesses of their hearts—if they have any—and say if Horace A. W. Tabor is not an open patron of prostitution, a diseased wreck, a mauled nonentity. An individual who solicits official honors without the ability to discharge the duties imposed. An individual [whose] whole notoriety is due to the efforts of subsidized journals and whose standing in society (?) attributable to a class who worship at a shrine which morality and intelligence will ever ignore. April 21, 1882

Henry M. Teller, United States Senator from Colorado, and then Secretary of the Interior under President Chester Arthur, continually aroused Day's ire. Nor did he like Jerome Chaffee, the other initial senator any better. Both were Republicans, a primary apprehension for Democrat Day.

Eventually he came to appreciate Teller, Colorado's premier politician of his generation and the state's leading silver advocate. Much to Day's pleasure, Teller ultimately switched parties over the Republicans' stand on the political "touch stone" silver issue.

When it comes to retiring Colorado politicians—so called, Mr. Teller is our first choice. Mr. T. is entirely too good a man to be contaminated by Washington Society. December 26, 1879

Senator Henry M. Teller as a Senator amounts to about as much as does the tray of clubs when hearts are trumps. October 1, 1880

Henry M. Teller is the most egregious ass that ever cursed the political stump of any state—a perfect non entity. September 24, 1880

Teller is a fraud. July 21, 1882

When Henry M. Teller endorses Henry C. Olney for Register of Lands at Lake City, he endorsed a thing that he himself voluntarily characterized as 'an individual unworthy of a public trust.' January 20, 1882

Teller has betrayed the wishes and confidence of a large portion of our people and the war will be bitter and to the point. January 20, 1882

Mr. Teller's endorsement of Henry C. Olney is just what we should have expected from a legislator of his caliber. Henry M. Teller by his endorsement of H. C. Olney has convinced us that as a free and voluntary liar he has no peer. January 20, 1882

The [Jerome] Chaffee boom is not destined to be the boom largest boom that has yet boomed in this booming country while there are so many b(u)mers. October 31, 1879

Will the people of Colorado elect a ticket born with J. B. Chaffee as the attending midwife, nursed on the bottle of federal interference and rocked in the cradle of infamy? Hardly. November 3, 1882

*Teller has repeatedly and consistently ignored this section.
March 17, 1882*

*The Muldoon's platform, free trade, free lunch, Pueblo, San
Juan and damnteller. January 20, 1882*

*Teller's name has not appeared on the Congressional Record
for eleven days. If he will just keep up the lick this constituency will be happy. February 24, 1882*

*If silence is golden, Henry M. Teller ought soon to be able to
liquidate the national debt. June 8, 1883*

*The Denver Times insists that Henry M. Teller is a credit to
the State. Henry M. Teller is a credit to greed, a credit to gall,
a credit to envy, a credit to willful prevarication and a credit
to all that tends to make monopoly and political tyranny a
success. Henry M. Teller is what the Muldoon calls a political wolf and voluntary liar. August 24, 1883*

*Senator Teller has declared himself a candidate for U. S.
Senator. But then, Henry M's candidacy cuts a very narrow
swath in this country. October 27, 1884*

*The Denver Times, in reviewing the senatorial contest
arrives at the conclusion that Henry M. Teller will do. But
when there is a demand for a stopper, and a cork in sight,
what in ---- is the use of hooking on to a corncob. November
28, 1884*

Colorado House Republican, James Belford, also received a
share of Day's remarks:

*Jim Belford is the tool of bonanza kings and not a fit man to
represent the industries of our state. October 22, 1880*

Belford is the most consummate hypocrite in all Colorado.
October 15, 1880

Mining man and politician, Thomas Bowen, actually made his fortune in San Juan mining, although on its southeastern corner at Summitville far from Ouray. In the 1880s, he joined other men angling for a senate seat and, in fact, beat out Tabor in the hotly contested 1883 contest.

> *The San Juan organs that speak, speak kindly of Tom Bowen, to say the least, are actuated by motives that are honest. Tom Bowen with all his faults, has not as yet, become so degraded as to stalk through this section for the sole purpose of sub-sidizing a press that will take anything from a meal ticket to a railroad pass. Mr. [Frederick] Pitkin this squib is direct square at the governor. September 1, 1882*

Colorado smelter man Nathaniel Hill also aspired for political success. Elected senator in 1879, he was up for reelection in 1886. Despite being a Republican, Day liked him because of his strong stand on the silver issue. He lost the election with Teller being returned to the senate.

> *There are only about two votes standing between silver and demonetization and one of the two is Senator N. P. Hill. Miners do your duty at the polls and don't allow the Ouray Pin Tails to win your suffrage one who has stood by the silver interest with all the ability and vigilance of a shrewd states-man and sound and fearless debater. October 24, 1884*

> *Of the eleven individuals opposed to the re-reelection of Senator Hill in Ouray county, not one can advance a reason for his opposition. January 2, 1885*

Dave Day later in life was active in politics.
Photo courtesy of Southwest Center, Fort Lewis College

Road builder, San Juan booster, and close friend of Day—Otto Mears found himself praised, and also "damned," for his Republicanism and lack of road maintenance. Of all the Colorado "movers and shakers" of this era, Mears became most associated with Ouray and frequently visited the community.

If Otto Mears would only put a few men in Blue Canyon to drain the water off the road and shovel out land slides it would be no more than his duty. Otto is in a fair way to get rounded up for negligence. May 7, 1880

The Muldoon *has said very many naughty things about Otto Mears, and is liable to say very many more, but the* Muldoon *has always commended that Otto Mears has done more for the development of the San Juan country than any other ten men in Colorado. To his wealth and energy Ouray owes a large share of the boom she is now enjoying. Otto is a shrewd, far-seeing business man, and an adroit and cunning politician, and a speculator of more than ordinary nerve and judgment. June 15, 1883*

Ouray county is now admirably equipped in the way of roads, having expensive thoroughfare on easy grades to Red Mountain, Sneffles, Uncompahgre and Poughkeepsie, and to Otto Mears we are almost absolutely indebted for the enterprises that have cost near two hundred thousand dollars. Mears is the San Juan "Pathfinder," and if there is any one individual or corporation in all this section that has done one-fourth as much toward developing this country as Otto Mears we are ignorant of the fact. October 3, 1884

Local elections could be just as heated as those statewide, and, in some way, they were much more emotional. Day, never one to stand on the sidelines or pull his punches, jumped right into the fray with his opinionated editorial pen. As would be expected, he neither held back nor quieted his views. Amazingly, he once even favored Republicans!

There will be county commissioners to elect this fall, and present incumbents suit this Muldoon exactly. Never saw a brace of republicans we were better pleased with and besides they are honest, and take great pride in looking after county affairs. April 18, 1881

The election Tuesday [town] was a very tame affair. The vote lighter than ever before and none, not even the old regulars, became sufficiently enthused to indulge in a plain drunk. April 9, 1880

Good men for town officers, and don't you forget it. March 5, 1880

SPLIT TAIL! The Democrats win all but 3 feathers . . . The Town Hall Scheme sot down on . . . A quiet election and won by good hard work [series headlines]
It is hoped that the 'thirteen chosen' who supported the town hall scheme will each try to kick himself in space or go off and sit down on himself. Thirteen who voted for a town hall when we have a rail pen for a school house, a dry good box for a court house and a corral for a jail. Who'd a think it? [vote 72-13] April 14, 1882

The election held Thursday night for the purpose of voting bonds for the erection of a ten thousand dollar schoolhouse was almost a one sided affair. Forty seven for, six against. November 10, 1882

Ouray is cursed with a gang who labor under the impression that they must be retained in office during their natural lives. They think the masses impotent to choose their public servants, and never miss an opportunity to push themselves forward. They have no political creed that is permanent, and their interests in advancement or welfare of any party depends solely upon their chances for office. The Muldoon is sick and sore of such presumptuous parasites, and trusts that the voters of both parties will sit down on them when the proper time arrives. June 22, 1883

The aim of the average Ouray county voter in the approaching contest seems to be gravitation towards the aid of responsible men, and not perpetual office seekers, as heretofore. There are, in this county, a gang of cranks who have, thro' the continued tender of the suffrage of this people, grown to believe that they alone are entitled to official revenue, and labor under the impression that the various county offices were created for their express use and benefit; and, ignoring the modesty that prompts men of worth and ability to halt, stick themselves forward for every office within the gift of the people. They are at the end of their rope, and the day has dawned when they will be compelled to rustle for an honest dollar, and stand back to make room for such servants as the people will, in their wisdom, elect. August 24, 1883

The voters of Ouray county have the necessary intelligence to select such official servants as they require for the next two years, and will do so without again calling upon the gang that now hold office. They have been tried and can show up nothing more conducive to prosperity than a receipt for salary. Give us a change, it is utterly impossible to do worse. September 28,1883

The present crop of Ouray politicians have been contemplating the organization of a S.O.B. club, but finding no hall large enough to meet the requirements abandoned the project. October 19, 1883

The average Ouray county republican views the democratic ticket in the light of a Christmas gift. The wretches. October 26, 1883

The Muldoon, in local politics, will be strictly cut and slash organ. The pintails can prepare their war paint, ours is already amalgamated and the color decidedly crimson. June 13, 1884

In an interesting 1881 election, the site of the state capital needed to be chosen. Because of the jealousy of Denver, the selection of a permanent state capital had been delayed for "no more than five years" when the state constitution had been written and ratified back in 1876. The first session of the state legislature set the date for1881.

When the time arrived a host of communities advanced their candidacy, each convinced it offered the perfect choice. This was not the type of issue that Day would sit still about, and, partly with tongue in cheek, he advocated Ouray.

At the next general election will be submitted to the voters of this great and prosperous commonwealth the question of a permanent location of the state capitol. Now it is highly possible some half-buttoned hamlet like Colorado Springs or Leadville may present the constituency, what they are pleased to term, 'our claims.' Mayhap Denver, with her dens of infamy, hells of iniquity, castles of rain, rotten politicians, state lotteries and opium dens, will have the sublime cheek to

"point with pride" to "our railroad center and other advantages." Fellow suffers . . . do you want the seat of government located in Denver? No. I repeat it in tones of unparalleled vengeance. And again, Colorado, like the Roman mother when asked to display her jewels, points with pride to Ouray and the Muldoon. Ouray, blessed Ouray, the gem of the Rockies, . . . a climate like unto that of Palestine, lovely grottoes, heavenly dells, verdant forests, beautiful river in whose placid bosom the dark-eyed maidens of the forest bathe...
[Day proposed Ouray] *Ouray blessed Ouray! Thou hast no dens of infamy to prison the legislative mind, no scarlet virgins to pray upon the law-makers salary. Ouray! Thou alone of all others should have the capitol. Yonder is the mecca. Let us strive for the tempting boon. December 3.1880*

Denver is almost certain to emerge for the capitol contest with a plurality. October 14, 1881

Denver will not get fifteen votes in Ouray county for the Capitol. Colorado Springs and Canon City will divide Ouray county's vote. Oct. 28, 1881

The voters of Ouray and vicinity, after a full, free and frank exchange of views on the Capitol question, have decided to waive all difference and combine on Canon City. It is very important to the people of the San Juan that the seat of Government should be located South of the divide, and in order to be successful in combating against our Northern neighbors, unity is essential. It is decidedly the most picturesque and appropriate point south of the divide and the advantage San Juan would derive by having the seat of Government located in the Arkansas valley are entirely too numerous and obvious to necessitate any itemized lengthy statement. November 4, 1881

We always did favor Denver for the capitol and exhibited our choice by walking up to the poles like a man and voting for--Canon City. November 18, 1881

Day could not resist humor on almost any occasion, and politics brought out some of his excellent quips and a few words of advice.

The churches were well filled Sunday evening—spring elections are approaching. January 27, 1882

The Democratic party in Colorado is in good fighting trim. It's the Republican liver that needs calomel. January 27, 1882

Next season the Muldoon will give politics a rest and go its length on mining news. We intend to paralyze Lake City and Silverton. December 22, 1882

A politician who comes to the point in pursuit of some coveted office is much more to be admired than one who sets around on the back fence waiting for a stray bone to be thrown his way. September 15, 1882

Some of Ouray's violent politicians differ from the hen inasmuch that they cackle before the egg is laid. March 31, 1882

CHAPTER 8

Utes

There was tragedy in the settling of these beautiful and rugged mountains. Someone was not welcome any more in the San Juans—the Utes who had lived nearby, hunted in the mountains, and marveled at the mineral springs for centuries. Now, their neighbors wanted them gone, the quicker the better. There was little new in all this, it had been occurring since the first Europeans arrived in North America over two war-filled centuries before.

From the start of the 1870s, trouble had been brewing. The 1873 Brunot agreement, allowing prospecting and mining in the mountains, had temporarily put a final reckoning on hold, but neither side seemed satisfied. The *Ouray Times*, from its very first 1877 edition, questioned why the Utes' reservation covered "some of the best land." That question evolved into "The Utes Must Go" by the time Day arrived.

From Ourayites' perspective, the Ute reservation blocked agricultural expansion into the "Garden of Eden" just north of them, threatened transportation in and out of the town, and severely impeded the growth of their community, its mines, and its future. Obviously something needed to be done.

One exception to this anti-Ute attitude existed, the highly respected Chief Ouray and his small band. At the time Day was planning his newspaper, Ouray and his people were welcomed and praised for, among other things, the vegetables "our red brothers" brought to town to sell. Even in the midst of the hysteria and hatred of the fall of 1879, the *Muldoon* still hailed Chief Ouray as a "voice for peace."

Then the inevitable finally happened. The White River Utes, located north near the future town of Meeker, killed their agent Nathan Meeker and eleven others. They also ambushed a column of troops that was on its way to support the agent, who had asked for help. That proved enough for Ourayites and their neighbors. They called for removal of all the Utes and demanded that troops be sent to protect them and remove these "enemies of progress."

The *Solid Muldoon* was just getting started when all this transpired and the "Ute War" broke out. Like other San Juan newspapers, its position was clear. The Utes most go. Once more, however, one exception existed, their namesake Ouray, who had rushed to end hostilities. Ouray managed to stop the fighting and help release captive women; but, while trying to bring about a permanent solution, he died in August of 1880.

Thus, Day and the *Muldoon* went to "war," but with a bit of humor now and then. For example on the third, "The entire *Muldoon* corps volunteered for the Indian war. This sudden gush of patriotism is expected to completely annihilate the Utes." The fun stopped right there, and woe unto those who spoke out in defense of these Native Americans. As usual, Day was not shy about presenting his attitudes.

However, the evolution of newspaper comments does show a change in attitude once the agreement to remove the Utes had been signed. Nonetheless, the "solution" was eagerly awaited.

The shortest route to a speedy settlement of the Ute question would be to withdraw the U.S. troops and turn the State militia loose. October 17, 1879

The honor of Colorado is at stake. Every red marauder engaged in the White River massacre should be hunted down and punished. The outside world must understand that there is a law to Colorado, the ability to enforce it. October 24, 1879

When Dave Day went to Colorado and started the Solid Muldoon *it was the last straw that broke the Ute's back. No wonder they were-stirred up. Sedalia News [Missouri] no date.*

Umph! Humph! Utes, when you catch David fooling around a 'Ute's back' with a 'straw' send him word. David hasn't lost any Utes, and besides, the country is fully prepared to suffer a national calamity. October 31, 1879

It costs the government only about $5,000,000 a year to support the Indians, but when we consider the pleasure the Colorado Springs Gazette *derives from their presence, we are not inclined to kick. November 7, 1879*

To the Governor of Colorado:
The undersigned citizens of the town and county of Ouray respectfully represent to your Excellency that the Indian troubles last fall prevented freighters from bringing in the usual winter supplies and that fear of the Indians still deters them until we are now suffering from a serious scarcity of the necessaries of life.
That this alarm is not unfounded will appear from the fact that no freight can be brought here except by bringing it through hostile Indian camps at the Los Pinos Agency. . . . Within the past few days Douglas, chief of the murderers and ravishers, has been furnished with provision at the Agency by a government which ought to hang rather than feed him. . . . [Petition signed by nearly every citizen of Ouray] *January 23, 1880*

The Utes are highly pleased with Washington [delegation there to sign another treaty]. *Well, we are perfectly willing that they should stay there. January 30, 1880*

Senator Teller has at last worked his gigantic intellect up to believe that the Utes must go. Everybody else in the state came to that conclusion last September. February 20, 1880

When the Indians are removed there may perhaps be a branch of the Union Pacific Railroad started from Rawlins and built south through the reservation to Ouray. February 20, 1880

To the Utes. Stand not in the order of your going, but go at once. February 27, 1880

The removal of the Utes is indeed a blessing, it enables Ouray to claim her place as the boss fissure vein camp of the state. March 12,1880

We are truly glad the Utes are to be removed, not so much on the account of the troubles they have caused as the prospect of getting rid of a mess of thieves who are a disgrace to civilization. March 12, 1880

Helen Hunt [Jackson] needn't chuckle because the papers have dropped her for a time. Select your Utes Helen; time's most up. April 16, 1880

On to the reservation: neither ask nor give any quarters. Sail right in and take the chances. [Farmers and ranchers were taking reservation land before it was opened] *April 30, 1880*

The Ute bill passed the house Monday the seventh inst. Let us join hands and circle to the reservation. June 18, 1880

The Utes are growing exceedingly friendly. Every day brings crowds of the red brothers to our village. July 2, 1880

The Utes have sold near a hundred ponies in Ouray this spring. The prices range from twenty-five to fifty dollars. Some of the animals offered are quiet, gentle and good saddlers, while others are capable of bucking off a postage stamp. July 9, 1880

*When the Utes were in their glory murdering the pioneer set-
tlers and burning their homes, the noble [governor] Pitkin
was sitting on the small of his back awaiting the pleasure of
an Interior Department Clerk. August 6, 1880*

*A dead Indian was found near the Big Bend [Dolores River].
From the bullet hole in his head it looked very much as if he
had been shot. Let the good work go on. November 5. 1880*

At last, blessed be the name of Schurz [Secretary of the
Interior Carl Schurz]—*the Indians under his charge are sure
enough farmers. According to his report they raised enough
hops last year to manufacture a glass of beer. December 10,
1880*

*Wouldn't it be a good idea to have the reservation opened
with appropriate ceremonies, such as breaking a bottle of
wine over Granny Schurz's head. Some character of vessel is
always chosen for such purposes. December 10, 1880*

*The Utes have signed a treaty for their reservation, have
received the money due them, and now have not interest
whatever in it. Go in boys and stake out a ranch. December
31, 1880*

*The Ute reservation will in the near future be the empire of
the cattle interests of the State. January 21, 1881*

*A squad of soldiers came up to Cow Creek last Saturday and
ordered several of the citizens of the park off their ranches
staked by them on the reservation. Like sensible men they
declined to go. Stick. February 11, 1881*

Utes and whites in a peaceful moment at the Ute Indian Agency on the Uncompahgre River.
Ruth and Marvin Gregory Collection

The settlers on the reservation are anxious for an excuse to clean out the Utes. If the Indians could be induced to kill some prominent white man it would be the signal for the utter extermination of the entire Ute tribe or at least so much of it as attempted to remain in Colorado. May 13, 1881

Among the Associated Press dispatches in the Pueblo Chieftain, *of the 10th, is one from Lake City to the effect that a "Ute outbreak is only a question of few days." In view of the fact that it is generally known throughout the state that there are five U.S. soldiers to every Ute warrior in the Uncompahgre Valley it is hard to tell which is the damndest fool, the originator of the dispatch; operator at Lake City; or the editor that publishes such sensation and unreliable gush. June 17, 1881*

Will the Colorado Springs Gazette, Pueblo Chieftain, Denver Times *and other papers that have displayed a vast amount of ignorance in locating the Indian troubles [Ute skirmish], please be kind enough to inform their readers that the fighting took place in Utah 190 miles from Rico, 221 miles from Durango, and 264 from Ouray. July 1, 1881*

Denver and Pueblo papers are doing more to injure the San Juan by locating the Indian troubles among us than all the wild cat mining schemes that have ever struck the country. July 1, 1881

The Uncompahgre Utes having been previously notified that they must vacate the valley and take up the line of march for their new reservation on the 25th, held their last and final pow wow at the Agency Wednesday p. m. August 26, 1881

The Utes, in this part of the county, are a thing of the past. And already the tide of immigration turns toward our beautiful and fertile valleys. September 9, 1881

The withdrawal of the cavalry and a large portion of the infantry from the Uncompahgre Valley will cause hay and vegetables to take a tumble in prices. September 9, 1881

The Ute question had now been resolved to the satisfaction of Day, his neighbors, and most Coloradans. All the bands, except the Southern Utes (already on a reservation), left for a reservation in Utah. Ouray had been able to convince the government that the Southern Utes had not been involved in the Meeker troubles and thus they stayed in and around Ignacio on their old reservation in the southwestern corner of the state.

With the opening of the Uncompahgre Valley, the town of Ouray's northern doorway was unlocked and now only awaited the coming of the railroad. With the establishment of Montrose, Delta, and other communities, plus farmers and ranchers settling throughout the valley, Ouray's need for an agricultural hinterland finally neared resolution. No longer would there be fears about food shortages or isolation.

The attitudes that the *Muldoon* displayed toward the Utes reflected that of many Coloradans and westerners, but not all. In her writings, Colorado Springs resident Helen Hunt Jackson tried to awaken Americans to the other side of the story, as did some easterners. Not so, said their western brethren. The Utes had been in the way of "progress" and America's "manifest destiny." They had to go—or so what seemed a majority of their neighbors ardently believed and proclaimed.

.

CHAPTER 9

Mining

uray owed its existence to mining. During the time of David Day and his *Solid Muldoon*, its principal tributary mines were located south of the community in the elevated Red Mountain district. Day paid close attention to developments, particularly to boosting Ouray's industry and its outstanding mines.

He did everything he could to promote local mining. The paper offered advice, including reports on individual mines, articles about visits to properties, production statistics, and general news of mining developments. Mills and smelters were desperately needed to separate gold and silver from the gangue, or waste rock. They arrived, but they also had to employ the correct machinery and process in order to successfully work Ouray ores. Often enthusiasm for an untried process left investors and miners with ruined hopes and empty purses. As can be imagined, all of this caught Day's attention.

However, he also remained vigilant in uncovering fraudulent stock, "wild cat" promotions, and exposing scams and their "wayward" owners, all of which threatened to give the district a bad name. Unfortunately, such incidents had happened far too often in many western mining districts, scaring away investors and potential buyers and leaving the district with a "bad taste" in its mouth.

Day attacked fraud, misstatements, "outright lies" and other nefarious schemes with his usual bluntness, mixing in a bit of humor along the way. No doubt, promoters and others failed to appreciate his sentiments.

The following article explains Day's view of mining operations. While every issue of the *Muldoon* carried some mining news or notes, the rather mundane accounts of production, ore coming into town, and trails being opened have not been included in this chapter.

'How Mining Should be Conducted'
    Legitimate mining should be conducted with the same rigid economy that renders mercantile transaction more liable to be successful. The miner certainly should whether the cost consists in the price he pays for a mine, or the expense attendant upon working it. If he pays an exorbitant price for the property, too much for the labor expended in its development, too high a price of the material used in prosecuting the work, he will soon learn by sad experience that by deviating from strict economy he has brought about his ruin.
    A disrepute has been cast upon mining by the reckless and careless manner in which investment have been made in mines. . . . no man works harder than the miner; no man strives more earnestly to obtain profitable results from his labors than does the miner; no man undergoes more privations than the miner; and no class of men meet with such general and continuous failure as the mining men. November 14, 1879

THE OSPREY CONSOLIDATED MILL & MINING COMPANY IS AN INFAMOUS AND DAMNABLE FRAUD. [headline] *November 21, 1879*

The Ouray Mining & Discovery company certainly offers a greater variety of chances than any other bonanza afloat. The only mistake they made was in not incorporating three or four ranches and a fishing privilege. *November 28, 1879*

The Osprey Consolidated Mill & Mining is a base bad fraud.
The Ouray Mining and Discovery Company will bear close and vigilant watching.
The San Juan & Poughkeepsie Gulch Mining Company, of Chicago, is playing above the limits.
The Muldoon proposes to canvass the merits and demerits of every company that places their stock upon the market. If

they are commendable we will take great pleasure in gratuitously promulgating the face. If they are not, the fur will fly.
December 12, 1879

Every attempt to bolster up a wild cat by a damage suit will prove an inglorious failure. Every effort to throttle the Muldoon *by threats or damage suit will go to the wall.*
December 19, 1879

THE OURAY TIMES *TAKES BACK ALL IT SAID IN REGARD TO THE OSPREY. WE HAVE BRANDED THE OSPRY AS A FRAUD AND WE TAKE BACK NOTHING.*
[headline] *January 9, 1880*

We are dead down on wild cat mining schemes, and don't you forget it. February 18, 1880

The Muldoon *has exposed and shown up more fraudulent mining schemes and "wild cat" mining companies than any other paper in the San Juan and will continue to keep up the lick until the last "varmint" is exterminated. March 26, 1880*

When a New York mining expert arrives in Ouray with letters of recommendation from 'prominent eastern capitalists,' he is given but four hours to skip, and he generally skips. April 2, 1880

We fully agree with the writer of a timely article in the Mining and Scientific Press *than there is a great want of custom mills and smelting works in almost every mining community; mills or smelters that shall be to the owners of mines what flouring mills are to the owners of the great wheat fields of the west and northwest; mills or smelters which will afford either reliable remunerative markets for the ore product of the vicinity or enable miners to have the results of their labor treated fairly and honestly for a reasonable consideration. April 16, 1880*

The Little Abbie Mining Company, capital stock $19,000,000, is said to be one of the slickest wild cats in all the San Juan. From parties who are acquainted with the property we learn that no ore that would pay the expenses of packing has ever been encountered. April 30, 1880

There is no capping in Mt. Sneffles [district], the pay streak in every mine that has been worked increases with depth. May 7, 1880

There is a greater demand for miners in Ouray county than in any other portion of the state. Mine owners are offering $3.50 and $4.50 per day and board the miners. We want them bad. [$3 and $3.50, with a dollar taken each day for board and room, was typical wages] *May 7, 1880*

Those miners who promised us specimens should not forget that we are still patiently awaiting their arrival. May 14, 1880

The value of specimen assays as a criterion of value in prospects and new mines is well understood by practical miners, but it is one of the most prominent inducements offered to the inexperienced by those who have mines for sale. It will be readily seen that a mine to be valuable must show something better than high assays from selected specimens. June 11, 1880

There is no mining camp in the state that has as bright and promising a future as Ouray. Our mines are not dependent on newspaper blowing for their richness. It's the ore on the dumps and in sight that does the talking. June 18, 1880

When the Little Abbie, Ouray Discovery and Mining Company, San Juan and Poughkeepsie Gulch company and the Mineral Point Tunnel mob have been mopped up this section of San Juan will be tolerably free from wild oats. July 16, 1880

Capitalizing prospect at one, five and ten million dollars is rapidly playing out. August 6, 1880

Some two weeks ago Mr. Geo. Schori paid us a visit and after giving the Muldoon *a vast amount of taffy he produced $5,000 of capital stock of the Germania company which he begged leave to present to us "as a testimonial of high regard etc." of the company he represented. Mr. Schoir's offer was peremptorily refused and he left soon after only to pursue the same tactic with the* Times *outfit and they in strict accordance with republican principles accepted the bribe—for it was nothing else—and in their next issue consummated the sale of the puny conviction in a laudatory notice of the Germania Mining Co.'s property. October 8, 1880*

[Star Milling & Smelting company] have certainly displayed more energy and enterprise in the transportation of their machinery and erection of buildings than usually afflict the average San Juan company. In rain, shine, sleet or snow, there is no cessation—the work goes on. November 12, 1880

If half the money expended for glittering prospectus of mining companies was expended in intelligent development on their prospective mines, it would be not half as hard to sell mining stock as it is at present. December 24, 1880

The Weekly Mining News *is unable to find the headquarters of the Riverside Tunnel Mining Company. Their tunnel*

*is up on Red Mountain. They haven't found their mine yet.
January 14, 1881*

*The approaching mining season will be the most prosperous
one of our Ouray county. Why almost everybody who owns a
mine wants to sell, it is what bothers the eastern people these
days. February 11, 1881*

The Solid Muldoon *invariably knows what it is doing when
it jumps a mining company. We have since we opened shop in
'79 tackled five and if any of them have recovered we know
it not. When we say a mining company is a fraud we are
always heeled with the necessary documents to establish the
fact. April 15, 1881*

*Dr. Hazard's concentrator is getting to understand the refrac-
tory nature of our ores and shows a disposition to settle down
to a fair and impartial treatment. There is no legitimate reason why the Doctor's machine should not be yielding him a
handsome revenue. June 10, 1881*

The Muldoon *has inaugurated a new industry, the manufacture of dynamite bombs for the extinction of high-toned and
glaringly magnificent mining frauds. August 5, 1881*

*Reports say that a big strike has been made in the Virginius.
If it is so why don't they say so? This heavy mystery business
is getting too previous altogether. The county needs all the
help it can get, but free publication of every good strike made,
and the concealment of them means either trickery or d---d
nonsense. September 16, 1881*

*The infamous fraud, the Ouray Discovery & Mining
Company is again "bobbing up serenely." October 21, 1881*

*The Muldoon will continue to perforate and expose all wild
cat mining schemes. The Bondholder and Bear Creek companies should take warning. We mean just what we say.
Ouray mines are sitting at the head of the table in New York.
Mt. Sneffels, San Miguel, Ophir and Bear Creek districts
are the richest in the state. That's what the mill runs say.
December 2, 1880*

*Mines may be run successfully and profitable unstocked, but
hell hath no fury like unto the novel feat of running stock
unmined. January 13, 1882*

*The Red Mountain section is creating a great deal of interest
now and many of Ouray business men are endeavoring to
obtain interests at that point. September 29, 1880*

*Red Mountain will be one of the best places to prospect next
season as exists in San Juan, and will be connected with Ouray
by a good wagon road so no time will be lost in converting ore
outputs into silver dollars. The stuff is there, is easily traded
and there is plenty of it. A boom will certainly visit the camp
and section next summer. November 10, 1882*

*The Muldoon man is slightly interested in Red Mountain
himself. What lovely and attractive millionaire we would
make. January 5, 1881*

*The Muldoon, since its inception, has carefully avoided all
gush and exaggeration when commenting on mines or districts, but development already justifies the assertion that Red
Mountain will certainly add millions to the output of Colorado.
In addition to the Yankee Girl, Hudson, Guston, Orphan Boy,
Genesse, and other mines of less development and notoriety,
new strikes are being made daily, and they are simply wonderful in point of quantity and richness. February 23, 1883*

The Red Mountain Mining District during its heyday about 1890-1900. Courtesy Southwest Center, Fort Lewis College

Red Mountain is unquestionably the Leadville of San Juan. February 23, 1883

The mines of Red Mountain are not exaggerated, the half has not been told. March 9, 1883

When you find an empty dump and 'No Admittance' over the drift or shaft house door, it is perfectly safe to gamble that there is a very large fraud very close by. April 20, 1883

We have been notified of three or four alleged mining companies that will work extensively this summer, but for fear they fail to make connection, will defer notice until the perspiration sets in. May 11, 1883

The towns of this district [Red Mountain] are almost entirely deserted. Only those are there who have actual business. The snow is from two to four feet deep, and lies in timber the sun cannot reach it. Prospecting is out of the question. Lake City Mining Register (no date)

Mr. Downey is respectfully informed that there are more men and more capital in Red Mountain than ever before and a great number of prospects are being developed than in the entire counties of Hinsdale and San Juan combined. May 25, 1883

There are a number of chronic cranks in the Red Mountain district, who are laboring under the impression that a stake stuck in the dirt, mud or snow, will hold a claim. Prospectors should pay no attention to such locations, as they amount to nothing and will not stand the racket even in a justice's court. June 11, 1883

The Yankee Girl and National Belle Dumps are a Sight Never before Witnessed in the History of Mining [headline]
Red Mountain is to-day the greatest and most wonderful camp on the continent. The entire district seems one mass of mineral, and strikes continue in rapid success. June 29, 1883

The mines of Red Mountain, Mt. Sneffles, Uncompahgre, Poughkeepsie, Mineral, Bear Creek, and portions of Engineer Mountain are directly and absolutely tributary to Ouray. August 31, 1883

Unfortunately, the Red Mountain District did not pan out initially as Day hoped despite his promotional efforts. It awaited investors with heavy cash reserves, mining engineers to resolve an amazing acid water flow problem, and the key, the coming of a railroad to lower costs and ease transportation. When all this happened, by the mid to late 1880s, despised rival Silverton, not Ouray, captured the trade and publicity. The main "culprit" was Otto Mears' Silverton Railroad, which reached the district, while no railroad from Ouray ever would.

Ouray will continue to sit at the head of the San Juan table and look after the banner. Our output entitles us to the position, and we can and will hold it. January 18, 1884

Over three hundred thousand dollars worth of ore piles in the ore houses of the Yankee Girl. Leadville can take the second place. August 1, 1884

Ouray county can show more ore on the dumps than any other county in the San Juan country. It is the Denver & Rio Grande railroad that we sigh for. August 15, 1884

Ouray county has added more to the annual yield of precious metals than San Juan, Hinsdale, Dolores and La Plata counties combined. January 2, 1885

The sudden interest and positive comments about the Red Mountain District just south of Ouray may have involved more than simply booming a district that Ouray planned to capture for her economic orbit. Day held mining interests there, a fact that he did not hide.

For all his comments about the vicissitudes and potential problems of mining, Day caught a case of "mining fever." The crusading newspaper man had high hopes just like anyone else, and "by golly," he won the "lottery." David and his partners sold the El Mahdi group on Dexter Creek in the Uncompahgre District, with Day receiving $40,000 as his share of the transaction. Not bad for a "rookie." Eventually he used his profits to travel to Europe to see the sights.

Mining reporting in the *Muldoon* decreased as mid-decade approached. This probably reflected the fact that Ouray County mining was growing out of its developmental stage and coming of age. Thus, it needed less local promotion, journalistic boosts, and pats on the back.

Not until 1883 would the county's silver production top $400,000 (actually a huge leap from $100,000, thanks primarily to the Red Mountain and Sneffels districts); then by 1885 it went over $900,000, definitely a major increase over previous years. Gold totals lagged far behind, in the $20,000 range. However, and it must have pleased Day, San Juan County's silver production ranged only in the $700,000s. These counties signified the top two producers in the San Juan District, with Hinsdale and San Miguel far behind.

Nevertheless, in comparison, booming Lake County averaged over nine million, and those two old-timers, Gilpin and Clear Creek counties, hovered at about two million. Ouray's day was coming, though, in the 1890s the county averaged around $1,000,000, and in the first decade of the new century, it broke the $2,000,000 barrier. At the same time, neighboring San Miguel ranged in the two to three million range, and long-despised rival San Juan topped $1,000,000 regularly and $2,000,000 occasionally. The faith of the "old-timers" had, at last, been generously rewarded.

By then the total production of the San Juans made it one of the great mining districts in American history as both a gold and silver district. David Day's predictions and expectations finally came to fruition, as well as those of a less vocal generation of San Juaners who had ardently believed in the mineral destiny of their mountainous region.

CHAPTER 10

Poetry

erhaps it is unfair to describe David Day's rhymes, doggerels, four line stanzas, and occasional several-verse adventures as poetry. His endeavors popped up every so often in the *Muldoon*, and, whether "borrowed" from other sources or original to him, he failed to say. Infrequently, Day did credit a known poet, but, at this late date, it honestly is hard to know who penned what.

Day did, however, frequently proclaim local people to be the authors, or less often some well-known Coloradan. Either way, readers were given a chuckle, unless, of course, they happened to be one of those acclaimed as "author."

He stood before the altar,
Leading the Sunday School choir;
After he'd sold his proxy for $25,
If he didn't, I'm a lyre.
—*September 5, 1879*

Backward, turn backward
Oh, time in your flight,
And make us a boy again,
Just for two nights.
—*November 28, 1879*

Tis rather neat upon your feet,
A pair of snow shoes to find;
Tis rather dear upon your rear,
When snow shoes flew up behind.
—*January 2, 1880*

Alas for pleasure on the deep,
And sorrows on dry land,
If $3.00 a gallon ain't too much for
Coal oil, may I be eternally—
—January 9, 1880

There was a young lady of Ouray
Who tried to ride on a sleigh;
She struck a stump
And fell off kerfump
And had a sore head the next day.
—January 30, 1880

It is better to coast and get a fall
Than not to try and coast at all.
—February 26, 1880

School house, school house we must have,
It's just what Ouray lacks,
So go to the meeting next Monday night,
And vote for the school house tax.
—February 27, 1880

In this cold world
We, do declare,
Nobody deals,
Upon the square.
—February 19, 1880

Other people have their faults
And so have we as well;
But all we see and hear and feel,
We dinna' need to tell.
—February 19, 1880

She may be homely and poor;
And her shoes number nine,
But if she is good and true,
She is the best valentine.
(Put that in your pipe boys and smoke it.)
—March 5, 1880

When lovely woman stoops to folly,
And finds too late that milk-men betray.
The injured spouse is eminently justifiable,
In packing his gripsack and moving away.
—April 9, 1880

Little Mabel's zebra stockings
Gently hang across the tub;
Brother George will find'em useful
When he starts his base-ball club.
—April 30, 1880

Around the bar-room stove I stand
And cast a watering eye
At those few lines above the bar –
No moni – no whiski.
—May 14, 1880

The last Methodist has faded and gone –
The last Presbyterian had fled,
And, the dear old Episco we loved so well,
Has packed up his gown and slid.
—May 14, 1880

Bet not on election,
For the cat may jump,
Not quite to your selection,
And leave you on a stump.
—November 5, 1880

When asked what Hancock carried,
Our sole reply shall be –
All of Las Animas,
And part of Missour – re.
—November 12, 1880

A young man may look very nice,
But if he happens to fall on the ice,
He drops all his airs, cur – es and swears,
And if anyone laughs, Lord! How he glares.
—December 17, 1880

Snow, snow, stop we pray –
Stop right off without delay;
Cease with so much ado,
We've might little use for you.
—February 11, 1881

He asked her if she loved him –
She chucked him 'neath the chin;'
He fondled and caressed her,
And then – oh' d—m that pin.
—March 4, 1881

When yesterday I asked you, love,
One little word to say,
Your brother interrupted us,
So please say yes-ter-day.
—June 3, 1881

Across the half-clad branches,
The mellow sunlight falls,
And I do believe, by jing:
There's a hole in my overalls.
—June 10, 1881

Mary had a vaccine scab
Upon her snow-white arm.
She warned her beau to this effect
For fear he'd do it harm

But when they came to part that night,
She gave a mighty grab,
And whispered, 'Hug me awful tight,
And never mind the scar.'
—July 8, 1881

The burro is a pretty bird,
And loves to dine on shirts;
And for a mid-day luncheon he
Prefers to eat old skirts.

Old petticoats and bloomers
Appraise his appetite;
While crinoline and corset stays
Fill him with great delight.
—August 5, 1881

We know a vagrant, worthless snipe – .
With a heart in hopeless mood –
Who hangs around full half the night
To steal the Muldoon's wood.
—September 30, 1881

Oh, how happy are they
Who their conscience obey,
And pay all their little bills soon.
No tongue can express,
How sweetly we rest,
When the cash rolls into the Muldoon.
—October 14, 1881

A damsel with kerosene
To the light fire did hope;
Next day, feet first, she left the house
In a rosewood envelope.
—November 18, 1881

Mary had a little lamb,
With which she used to tussle,
She pulled the wool all off its back
And ram-med it in her bustle.

But when he saw he had been fleeced
He in a passion flew,
So Mary got upon her ear
And stuffed the lamb in too.
—November 25, 1881

I went to the ball looking
As bright and fresh as a rose,
But ere the racket had faded,
I had it, 'upmynose.'
—November 25, 1881

Many a shot at random sent,
Finds aim the archer never meant.
—December 9, 1881

Hold me tight, don't let me fall;
I won't be afraid at all.
—December 9, 1881

The man who loves not,
Women, wine or song.
Will never die of bright's disease,
Or an over dose of fun.
—December 16, 1881

He faced the deacon like a lion;
And y-e-s like a grown man;
Has settled down to business,
And don't give - - - - -.
—December 16, 1881

As the *Muldoon* entered 1883, Day published fewer poems over the course of a year. Another change appeared. The subjects now became more locally oriented, with the name or names of the "authors" generally included with the poem.

This must have amused *Muldoon* readers, but leaves later readers wondering what created the background for his poetic literary efforts. It also brings up the question as to whom and why the "victims" received such a "literary honor." The names of people little known today have not been included. Those stanzas focusing on unclear local issues have been left out, as have those he previously used and used again by changing only a word or two.

The office's closed, I'll take a stroll –
Although tis rather late –
But soon you'll see me with my girl
A swinging on the gate.
—January 6, 1882

Little deeds of kindness,
Little words of love,
Make the old folks pleasant
And mash their youngest dove.
The melancholy days have come.
—January 20, 1882

The man who cheats the printer,
By not paying for his papaire,
Will surely reach that awful place
Where Lazarus struck the millionaire.
—May 4, 1883

One by one the boys all do it
One by one they marry off.
Some win joy and ne'er regret it;
Others 'pass' a female 'bluff.'
—March 17, 1882

There is a picture that haunts me ever:
Lips like cherries—ripe and rare;
Kissed by another, now, I suppose,
What does it matter—I had my share.

We loved. How true.
I lied,
As lovers do –
She cried.
One we trusted –
Thought each other true;
Now we're busted,
I've none to cling to.
Now I wonder
Who in thunder
Clings to her.
—March 17, 1882

In the spring's fancy
Lightly turns to thoughts of love.
And the young man with his Nancy
Loves in shady wood to rove.
—May 26, 1882

There was a young man from Montrose
Who raised quite a smell with toes.
It is hard on the nose
Of the girls and beaux,
For the feet will smell bad till it snows.
—August 4, 1882

Oh, d—d the flies, the little flies
They buzz around your head;
But soon the chilly nights will come,
And freeze them 'em all stone dead.
—September 8, 1882

Mary had a little lamb,
She bought it very cheap,
And when it tired of being a little lamb
It grew into a sheep.

It followed her to town one day,
And didn't know what to think
When it saw folks all round
Inside the skating rink.

Then said the sheep 'tis deuced queer
What the devil can have got 'em?'
Just then poor Mary tripped and fell
And bumped her little – head.
—December 15, 1882

The saddest of the year;
Old Fritz has to shovel snow
To earn his daily beer.
—January 5, 1883

You bet they do, and parlor fires
Are better far by roods
Than red ants up your trouser legs,
At picnics in the wood.
—January 12, 1883

And with the lamp turned safely down,
Your girl upon your knee,
Is much of ahead of moonlight hugs,
Or kisses 'nearth a tree.'
—January 12, 1883

In spring, the sap ascending,
Swells and bursts the fragrant rose;
In spring, our dandy Sheriff,
Takes a tumble on his nose.
—May 4, 1883

NO word was spoken when they met
By either—sad or gay;
And yet one badly smitten was,
As was remarked the next day.
They met by chance this autumn eve,
With neither glance or bow;
They often came together so –
A freight train and a cow.
—May 25, 1883

Across the verdant branches,
The mellow moonlight falls;
And I do believe, by jingo,
I've struck a match, after all!
—July 6, 1883

Our own M. Diller
Leaned back to the piller,
But the piller wasn't around;
Madly grasping his chair,
Wildly clutching the air,
He ignominiously came to the ground
And that's what's the matter of Diller.
—July 27, 1883

In the Spring the pensive chipmunk
Takes a pard and builds a nest
In the spring the gentle bed-bug
Tickles the leg that tastes the best.
—March 21, 1884

The saddest words of tongue or pen,
The saddest these. I'm me busted again.
—April 4, 1884

The June bug has a tinted wing,
The lightning bug a flame.
The bed bug cuts not such a dash,
But 'get there all the same.'
—July 25, 1884

Just as he was, without one plea
Save that love's blind and cannot see
Which way to go, unless his guide
Shall be a winsome, loving bride.
—September 6, 1884

He struck it rich, you bet your life,
When he found the Herma Goodell mine
He'll see no more bad times or strife,
For life's prospect to him is fine.
—September 26, 1884

The mail-ancholy days have kum,
The saddest of the year,
When ye editor, for want of clippings,
Fill up on—bottled beer.
—Dec. 26, 1884

CHAPTER 11

Godliness
and
Sinfulness

Writers and journalists often portrayed western mining camps as lost to respectability, Victorian values, and morality. That, no doubt, lured a share of their readers to delve into the story and maybe even journey west to sample the fun times and sin. On the other hand, more than a few easterners thought missionaries and good Christians of any stripe should be sent westward to save wayward "souls" and restore decency before the "plague" spread.

Locals, on the other hand, while realizing the need for a red light district—saloons, parlor houses, cribs, and gambling "hells" (features in a male dominated world)—hoped to project a more civilized, and respectable life style. After all, they wished to convince visitors, investors, and potential settlers that Ouray resembled its older, urban counterparts in the more settled parts of the country back in the East and Midwest.

In the transitory world of mining, however, criminal activity remained a fact of life. In his own inimitable way, Day reported the crime scene and the other shady events and personages in his hometown.

The man who would steal charcoal must indeed be a wretch.
March 12, 1880

Monday a. m. Shaveno accompanied by his son and other Utes drove in from the agency in their carriage and desiring to spend the night in Ouray the horses were unharnessed and harness deposited underneath the carriage in front of Mears' hardware store. During the night some infamous wretch with out fear of the wrath to come before him stole the entire out-fit. Shaveno was of course considerably worked up over the affair, but not any more so than the good people of Ouray. May 21, 1880

Each succeeding day brings additional complaints of undue [claim] jumping, an abdominal practice that must be expected to continue in vogue until the miners of Ouray and vicinity organize for self protection. July 9, 1880

Quite a number of our citizens are sleeping with their boots within reaching distance—burglars. March 4, 1881

Wife beating, and cruelty to women may be tolerated in more pious states of the east, but here in Ouray, where sin and the Muldoon hold high carnival, it can not, and shall not exist. We always make it a religious duty to interfere in behalf of the weaker sex as there are no circumstances under which a man is justifiable in cruelly mistreating a woman. A word to the wise etc. July 1, 1881

The members of the city council are considerably exercised over the disposition shown by the "soiled doves" to run the machine. [quotes bawdy house ordinance] The duties of the council in the premises are plain. They should either enforce the ordinance, revoke it, or move out. There is no half way grounds and the reason assigned for non-enforcement is the shameful report that one of our pure and pious city officials is guilty of violating the "contribute to its supports" section. August 26, 1881

It almost breaks our poor heart to think that a courtesan would become so lost of all sense of decency as to lure one of the pure inspirit from the paths of virtue and morality. We shall see what we shall discover. August 26, 1881

Can it be possible that one of our town officials is guilty of conduct unbecoming to the head of a family and is afraid of exposure in enforcing the "bawdry house" ordinance? August 26 1881

And now, among other misdeeds we have to chronicle, the stealing of two horses from Elephant coral last night. Surely Ouray needs her Vigilantes. September 2, 1881

The "doves" at the corral wear a rock in their silk wipes, give them a wide berth boys. September 30, 1881

The female of easy virtue, who attempted suicide last week at 220 [saloon/crib], left for sunny Pueblo, accompanied by her male attendant. November 4, 1881

Ouray county comes to the front with another murder. Blessed or blasted Ouray which? June 2, 1882

Two men killed in Leadville. One ahead of Ouray with Placerville and Dallas to hear from. June 9, 1882

When these thieving wretches become so bold as to enter a house in the evening and compel a helpless woman to cook them supper, as was done Mrs. Murphy Tuesday evening, then it is time to rid the town of that stripe of character. Damaboom if that element must accompany it. October 6, 1882

The reckless manner in which the soiled doves settle around in various portions of our once moral village should at least suggest a herd law. Let the evil be concentrated or bounced. February 16, 1883

Females of questionable habits and surface morals are settling down in localities where virtue abounds; leaders of society have subordinated the waltz and drama to Sunday horse racing; pillars of the church and statesmen, who were once the pride and envy of our village, have fallen victims to the seductive wiles of s. h. poker [Stud Horse Poker] and other worldly amusements. Shame! Shame! Shame! March 9, 1883

It is decidedly mortifying to note the rapid increase of drunkenness among the member of the Ouray bar. Shame, shame, shame! March 28, 1883

The [Alfred] Packer trial is progressing in Lake City. P. S. the Ouray county Commissioners have a scaffold for sale at actual cost. April 13, 1883

Two of Ouray's erring damsels engaged in a pugilistic picnic Saturday night at the Dance Hall. Marshal Harris would have locked them up had not bail been secured. Girls! Girls! April 20, 1883

Wednesday evening a pistol matinee took place at Hess's sample rooms, between Mike Flanagan and Joseph Victti, two Virginius miners. The weapons used were .38's and number of shots exchanged four. The participants escaped without bloodshed, but a bystander, Henry Williams, was severely wounded in the wrist. The affair was more attributable to whiskey than malice, and Justice Long fined each one hundred dollars and cost, which was promptly paid. April 20, 1883

It grieves us to notice the amount of dissipation the young men of our camp indulge in. County officials get stone blind; middle-aged men with families in the far east have to be carried home on a shutter; while young men whose parents back in Michigan and Wisconsin, are nightly involving the hidden hand to protect their dear ones from snow-slides and mountain lions, walk up to the bar and call for straight whiskey with as much indifference as a grown man. Nice town for a God-fearing, law-abiding father to raise a family in. May 4, 1883

We trust our resident ministers will exert every effort to prevent the youth of our city from indulging in those sinful exercises that render this life disgusting, and destroy all hope of a bright and blessed future. It will require a week of prayer to reclaim our county officials. May 4, 1883

Never has a man died in Ouray with his boots on. We preserve the reputations of our village by chasing the bad men beyond the corporate limits before the six shooter act. September 21, 1883

The breaking of a lamp caused an incipient blaze in Fay's sample rooms on Wednesday evening. Unfortunately no tinhorns were scorched. May 18, 1883

The stallion poker mechanics have been very judiciously treated to a grand bounce. They are simply a draw back to any and all camps that will tolerate them. June 27, 1884

Several plain drunks were anchored in the calaboose Sunday night. Most of the inebriate wretches were from Michigan and Indiana. Hard lot of citizens those States are sending west. June 22, 1884

Ouray county has managed, by the aid of a well organized vigilance committee, to keep the city jail empty for nearly a year. The bad men give Ouray a wide birth. July 4, 1884

The Muldoon *desires to go on record as opposed to that species of larceny known as "stud-horse poker"* [five card stud], *and those who threaten to withdraw their patronage on account of our position, are welcome to stop at once. There is no policy in this shop, and we stand in with an element that has supported the town in darker hours. Ours is a black flag. July 25, 1884*

The rush of tramps, tin-horns and adventurers to Silverton, Telluride and adjoining camps has increased the supply of hold-ups and rendered life a burden in those camps. Here in Ouray our city council wisely and judiciously weeded out the riff-raff, and we are moving along as serene and placid as a Siwatch bride. Ouray always did manage to run herself without aid of any violent consumers, beats or stragglers. August 22, 1884

When the Red Mountain Review *says that gambling of any kind "'tis generally considered to be a leading feature of a mining camp," it simply is making a ---- fool of itself. September 12, 1884*

The gambling craze seems to have broken out again, and some who aspire to positions in social and political life, have become so lost to all surroundings and the ordinary sense of shame as to sit at the gaming table night after night with the brazen indifference of a tin-horn. October 24, 1884

Apparently, not a particularly religious man himself, Day understood, however, the value of churches to mining communities. They improved the camp's image for the visitor, offered women and children social outlets not otherwise available, looked beyond the daily materialism for life's higher meanings, and did try to improve the morality of the general populace. All-that aside, he also at times poked a bit of fun at church members and churches and was not above chastising them on occasion. Even after he moved to Durango, he published this comment in the June 8, 1906 issue of the *Democrat*—"Sunday baseball is preferable to the average Sunday sermon."

The duty of the church falls upon the Muldoon. *Well, we are no respecter of persons and would just leave tackle an orthodox hypocrite as an avowed sinner. Bring in the victims. April 20, 1880*

Parson [C. N.] Hogue has gone to Rico prospecting carbonates and sinners. May 7, 1880

The Fair and Festival given by the lady friends of the M. E. Church, on Friday evening of last week, was socially and financially a success, netting $135. The display of fancy articles in needlework, etc., was indeed attractive, more especially so when we consider that but a short time was given for preparation. November 26, 1880

Religion is retrograding in Lake City and Silverton, but here in Ouray where the Muldoon *carries the banner of piety, it is just a boomin'. June 17, 1881*

The Methodist festival at the Dixon [House] Wednesday eve was beyond doubt the most successful church event of the season. The lord's chosen people enjoyed the creams, bon bons and social mélange until the Rev. W. H. Green and his lady departed for their home. When the sinners subsidized 'Gideons ban' and then, O-o-o then. June 17, 1881

The present choir of the M.E. church is certainly an excellent one. Miss Crotzer, the accomplished organist, assisted by Uncle Newhall with his fiddle, furnish the talented vocalists with splendid accompaniments. In fact the choir would not be replete with a single member missing. December 2, 1881

And now there comes rumor of a scheme to make automaton (sic) preachers. A very good idea. It would certainly be an improvement on the average minister and would not be so expensive. December 16, 1881

It reminded us of the old brick church way back on the virgin soil of the eastern states to see the goodly number of gallants and their pretty charming companions at church last Sunday evening. Do some more. December 23, 1881

This has been a week of prayer with Protestant denominations. Lookout for a severe storm next week. January 6, 1882

Rev. A. Scotland draws the boys out with his short and entertaining discourses. Long, windy sermons don't interest in this section. February 3, 1882

The Rev. Scott who has been preaching in Gunnison for the past two years to the M. E. church arrived in Ouray Monday to take charge of the M.E. church here. Rev. Scott is a zealous and untiring worker and will do much toward redeeming the waning light in Ouray. September 8, 1882

The Pueblo clergy are howling vigorously against Sunday amusements. Excursions and other harmless and health giving exercises are bitterly denounced. A proper observance of the Sabbath should be maintained in every community. But this thing of adopting or trying to enforce the blue stocking or puritanical code the west will not connect. There is less harm and more Christianity in buggy or boat riding on Sunday than there is in remaining indoors and quarreling with your wife or slandering the neighbors. June 23 1884

On Sunday night at the Episcopal Church Parson Knapp will deliver a discourse on "respectable sin." And the Muldoon *trusts that those of our wives and mothers who are afflicted with susceptible husbands, will prevail upon them to attend. January 11, 1884*

It is indeed a sad commentary on the Christian religion when our resident ministers are forced to follow down either side of the river on each succeeding Sabbath in order to tap the deacons and more humble members of the fold for the regular monthly collection. Heavens, how the trout do bite. May 23, 1884

The recognized religion of to-day is for rich and fashionable sinners. The poor and poverty stricken, who in the blessed by, "heard gladly," the discourses of the Nazarene are shown a back pew, or furnished with a knot hole. October 26, 1884

Dave Day enjoyed holidays, with Christmas being one of his all time favorites. This showed a sentimental streak in the editor that, perhaps, he would just as soon not have surfaced; but, like the redeemed Scrooge, "It was always said of him, that he knew how to keep Christmas well, if any man alive possessed the knowledge."

Notwithstanding the severe snow storm of the past week, Old Santa Claus got in on Wednesday eve. Two elegant trees, one at the Methodist, and the other at the Presbyterian church awaited him.

Everything passed on pleasantly and all went feeling the better for having been present. Merry Christmas to all. December 26, 1879

On Christmas day, Saturday, at the Episcopal church, there will be a morning service, with music and sermon, at 11 o'clock. Let all attend.

Christmas will be observed by the citizens of Ouray in various ways. There will hardly be a table in town that will not be graced a turkey or chicken. Several families will have private trees, while the union tree at the Episcopal church will have a present for every child in town. Those intending to take presents to their friends are cordially invited to hang them on the tree. December 24, 1880

It is safe to say that the day [Christmas] will be remembered for many succeeding months. To men undergoing hardship and toils in the pursuit of wealth, Christmas day comes to remind them of the one cherished treasure of life, his childhood's home. The burly stalwart miner may forget many things, but they never forget the prayers lisped at the mother's knee, and though she may have gone to her ever lasting holiday at each succeeding Christmas day, the veil is lifted and their hearts become more tender and thoughtful. December 31, 1880

Christmas day dawned drearily, the clouds hung in dull laden colors. About noon it began to snow in a weary lackadaisical way, and continued at regular intervals during the day. The

streets present a desolate appearance until about 9 o'clock
when might be seen the laughing faces of happy children running hither and thither comparing presents; men with haggard
looks caused by too deep worshiping at the shrine of Thomas
and Jeremiah, parents with depicted pocket-books and scull-
ing faces. Everybody seemed to be in their best humor and
bent on making each other happy. The saloons did a rushing business all day, Tom and Jerry, egg nog and San Juan
paralyzer being the favorite beverages . . . . In the Episcopal
church rector, Rev. E. P. Cross, preached an appropriate sermon to a large congregation. The singing was exceedingly
enjoyable while the tasteful decorations of the church added
charm. December 31, 1883

A few of the 'bloods' were what we are pleased to term dis-
gracefully drunk on Christmas. We do not object to a reasonable amount of hilarity, but when one becomes so lost to all
surroundings as to defy common decency, we think it time to
call a halt. December 29, 1882

In the midst of all these Christmas festivities let not the poor
escape your memory. Contributions of a perishable and liquid
nature should be delivered to the editor in person. December
29, 1882

If it is intention of the of the good ladies of Ouray to generally observe the custom of keeping open house on New Year's
day, we would be glad to have all who so intend, to send
their names to the Muldoon office, giving the hours between
which they will be pleased to see their friends.

This will greatly convenience the gentlemen and prevent
them from bumping against any basket on the door knob.
December 19, 1879

Dave Day got his photograph taken with his grandson.
Photo Courtesy of Denver Public Library

Other holidays and special dates also caught his attention and pen. Dave Day never was one to miss any of them.

GE-LORIOUS FOURTH

The fourth passed off to the queen's taste in this section of the vineyard. The joy was uncorked early Saturday morning and continued without cessation until Monday night. Ouray pulled through with one plain knockdown and several ditto drunks. In the park below town horse racing between the whites and Utes began early Sunday morning and continued throughout the day, the Utes, as usual, coming out ahead. July 9, 1880

Could G. Washington, Esquire, have dropped into Ouray last Tuesday, and witness the masquerade given in honor of his anniversary, . . . he would smiled a smile of bless satisfaction. The affair in addition to being the finest ever given in Ouray, was certainly the most unique, in point of costumes and general make up, ever given in any country. In large towns where costumes can be procured for a nominal sum, masquerading is not so difficult, but, here in far off Ouray where lords and lady's inventive genius are turned loose...it becomes interesting to know what to wear and how to wear it. Of the 114 costumes worn, 110 were strictly of home manufacture. February 25, 1881

This is Lent, and we trust the followers of the Episcopal creed will abstain from all worldly amusement during the sacred period, and give us sinners a chance to get a partner for the first set. February 29, 1884

The custom of throwing in a dollar on Easter Sunday to be used as the parson thinks best is a good custom. The Muldoon *man sent his up. Don't forget boys, that dollar, that, the parson knows exactly what to do with it, and Easter comes but once a year. April 11, 1884*

Yesterday was St. Patrick's day and many were the prayers that went up for suffering Ireland. March 18, 1881

The President has declared Thursday November 24 as a day of national thanksgiving and prayer. Turkey catches us more than the praying part. November 18, 1881

The Thanksgiving dinner to be served in Wright's Hall promises to be the feast of the season. The bill of fare will embrace all the solid luxuries and nick-nacs that the markets of the state affords. Turkeys, chickens, venison, grouse, salads, oysters, celery, cakes, creams etc., and all for the sum of seventy-five cents. November 24, 1882

As this will be the last issue of the Muldoon *prior to Thanksgiving let us not forget the following blessings that have been showered upon the people vis, to-wit: The Red Mountain road, Muldoon, each and every issue . . . two-fifths of the Town Board; that bridge down by the brewery; the new school house. November 23, 1883*

To-morrow will be Arbor Day and property owners should not overlook the shrubbery. April 25 1884

Arbor Day was not a howling success in this section, it is only on St. Patrick's and Bock Beer occasions that our people enthuse. May 2, 1884

CHAPTER 12

Baseball, Cats and Other Things

One of the aspects which made the *Solid Muldoon* so interesting to its readers was the fact that David Day possessed capacious interests in everything around him. This chapter samples some of his journeys into the multiplicity of life in a mining town as seen through the eyes of its "favorite" citizen.

A game of base ball is like a buckwheat cake—a great deal depends on the batter. February 25, 1881

Any man who has had his nose flattened or his thumb driven up his elbow can flatter himself that he has helped to open the base ball season. April 2, 1881

Base ball is all the rage and when it comes down to crack players we have some that are hard to scoop. April 7, 1882

Base ball seems to be growing in favor. It is more pleasant than chopping wood and equally as healthy. April 21, 1882

The Ourayites will endeavor to muster up a nine to accommodate the Cantonment base-ball club [soldiers stationed north of town during the Ute troubles] *on the 10th. Hazard, Home, Worthington, Rich and others will participate. "Shorty" Davis will be used for home base, and Luther Harris for a foul strike. June 29, 1883*

The game between the Cantonment and Ouray clubs in the Park, Tuesday, resulted in a victory for the Ouray boys, the score standing 25 to 9 at the close of the sixth inning. Time of game three hours. The playing in several instances, especially fielding and fly-catching was good, while throwing to bases and stopping "daisy cutters" exceedingly indifferent. The Cantonment boys did splendidly the first two innings, but it was evident that they had not the wind and began to exhibit an indifference, but walking after the ball, etc that was anything but commendable. They gave up after the sixth inning and acknowledged their inability to cope with the drill-pounders from the hills. Wallace, as Umpire, gave satisfaction and everything passed off pleasantly. July 13, 1883

The Ouray base ball club would have got in one or two more runs had not the horrible Cantonment Umpire acted so dishonorable. He actually refused to allow the boys to catch flys in their hats. The wretch. There will be a match game of base ball between the benedict and gum suckers of the Ouray social club next. Admission free. No bouquets will be received until after the third inning. May 30, 1884

The base ball game between the "Junior" and the "Virginius" boys on Sunday resulted in a victory for the latter. The boys play very well as long as they are ahead, but when defeat begins to loom up their pitcher gets sick and the first baseman finds fault with his abdomen. But children will be children. July 11, 1884

The game of base ball played Sunday was the best of the season. The score standing 17 to 23, and the number of whitewashes, three. The fielding was good, and the fly catches way up. August 15, 1884

Silverton's base-ball club is anxious to play the Ouray, Telluride or Rico clubs, for one hundred dollars. We are in favor of Ouray getting up a nine and tackling those polar region fellers. August 29, 1884

The base-ball game on Monday resulted in two broken fingers, a sprained ankle, crippled back and a score that stood seven to nine. August 29, 1884

The essay upon the "secrets and sanitary advantages of base ball upon the muscular system," by Prof. Tim. Gibson was crowded out this week, and the Prof. himself is not, strictly speaking, so sure about the views set forth in the aforesaid essay as he was. August 29, 1884

To-day the Ouray baseball club will go to the Cantonment to play the "Blue-legs" another match game. We hope, for the sake of the Ouray club's reputation, that they will get at least half as many scores as the b-ls. September 5, 1884

The base ball boys will provide seats for the ladies to-morrow afternoon. All are invited. September12, 1884

The Ouray nine rattled the Cantonment base ball club nearly two to one on Saturday afternoon, and after beating the boys proceeded to deluge them with a species of hospitality that produced partial paralysis. Soda on the side. September 19, 1884

The hunting and fishing in Ouray county was never so good. There is world of bear, deer and sheep and the streams are surfeited with specking beauties. August 5, 1881

One of Ouray's many semi-professional teams, circa 1920. Ruth and Marvin Gregory Collection

Fishing parties are now in order, but the trout do not seem to be as hungry as they were this time last season. But, this is an off year for the San Juans. July 25, 1884

Our business streets are usually lined with curs that are continually fighting and making day and night hideous with their yelping. Can't the town board get rid of this nuisance. Load up some of our 'wind suckers' and kill off a few of the mongrels. March 31, 1882

There is nothing so refreshing to tired nature as to sit at one's chamber window and watch a burro trying to recite Pope's "Wife of Bath." The fourth verse generally produces mental aberration. July 29, 1881

The mule that disturbed us so last week commenced his serenade again this week and just as it was getting down to mellow ninety-day-promissory-two-percent we fired—actually fired—a bootjack at the reptile, whose voice immediately rose to high G then melted away in a low, mournful cadence which echoed and re-echoed through cliff honed canons and wooded dells as it was wafted on the crisp health giving air of about 4 a. m. and thus do burros make heroes of us all. September 29, 1882

The marshal will enter upon the ghastly duty of exterminating four-legged dogs on Monday, and continue from day to day, until all that portion of the canine family upon whom tax is not paid are dead, dead, dead. May 18, 1883

Two dog fights were the only excitement in town Wednesday. January 23, 1885

We want a strong bellows-lunged, able-bodied rooster, one that will commence crowing at midnight keep it up until the gong sounds. It is the Corbott family we want to get even with. March 30,1883

When a cat gives an entertainment from the top of the wall, it isn't the cat we object to. It's the waul. January 30, 1880

The statement going the rounds that a cat can not live at an altitude of 13,000 feet is false. The cat at the Virginius mine, in addition to retaining a prime article of health, has found time to raise an interesting family of kittens. The Virginius, 13,320 feet. May 26, 1882

One of Dad Town's girl cats is bothering the life out of those Sanderson boys nights having taken up its residence under the stage office where it receives gentlemen cat callers. Oct. 13. 1882

White cats have superseded pugs and poodles among the fashionable dudes. When absurdity discards the immaculate feline and adopts the "white owl" then we will be O.K. October 19, 1882

Occasionally, Editor Day poked some gentle fun at the ladies. Probably along the way, a complaint or two came his way.

Women have no worse enemies than women.
Woman is a creature between man and the angels.
Women like balls and assemblies as a hunter likes a place
*   where game abounds.*
Women who have not fine teeth only laugh with their eyes.
Woman is a charming creature who changes her heart as
*   easily as she does her gloves.*
A beautiful woman is a paradise of the eyes, the hell of the
*   soul, and the purgatory of the purse. May 27, 1881*

The latest style of hats for ladies are said to be large enough to play hide-and-go-seek around. November 18, 1881

Announcement of Marriage. A.C. Yost to Miss Winnie Monney. No Cards; no cake; no invites; nobody dropped on in until all was over. December 16, 1881

The ladies view the grand Army supper in the light of a burlesque. Beans, hardtack, bacon and coffee do not seem to meet the approval of those who didn't follow Sherman from Atlanta to the sea. July 27, 1884

The ladies of the Episcopal Church have organized for the summer a campaign against sinners. They will devote their energies to rescuing miners and editors, as experience has taught them that lawyers and bank cashiers are not worth saving. March 13, 1885

Dave Day was ahead of his time in one respect, concerning what today are described as environmental issues. To his generation, and those before, the land and water existed primarily to be utilized for personal development and gain. Without question, this was part of the American Dream. Since 1607, advocates proclaimed that the opening of the West to progress and profit benefited the country as a whole, as well as individuals.

Unfortunately, utilization of the West's natural resources most often happened with little or no regard to current and future consequences. This included setting forests afire to clear the land for prospecting, and dumping waste rocks and trash in or near streams. The result, time and again, ended with polluted streams, litter scattered across the countryside, smoky air, and the landscape scarred and battered as prospectors and miners raced about digging after the elusive gold and silver. Day called attention to the problems on several occasions, including one long and, for the time, perceptive editorial.

The atmosphere is pregnant with smoke from forest fires on the Dolores [River]. Hanging two or three scamps for pure cussedness and carelessness should tend to discourage such infamous business. June 18, 1880

When Prof. Rossiter W. Raymond [former United States Mining Commissioner] visited this country he expressed his wonder at the cruel way in which the beautiful timber, that clothes our hills, is being destroyed, and no wonder! But as Boss Tweed [New York City politician] used to say, "What are you going to do about it."

Every new mining camp has its quota of tenderfoot prospectors and campers who never dream of putting out the fire when they leave in the morning and with a light wind and dry leaves in twelve hours more than hundreds of acres of magnificent pine trees are charred sticks. Then there are always a few Goths and Vandals who care nothing for the future of the country and think it fun to "start a fire."

Mr. Raymond also expressed his conviction that in all probabilities some day thousands of dollars would be spent in Ouray by tourists and sight-seers who, when the railroad is completed, will visit our town for the lovely scenery, hot springs etc. No doubt he is correct, and ought we not, therefore, to make some effort at least to preserve the timber that adorns the sides of our superb amphitheatre. It is now being rapidly cut down for firewood, and a year or two more of such ruthless destruction will render Ouray an eye-sore instead of the charming, picturesque place it now is.

Of course we must have a supply of firewood, but let it be brought from below town and not from the hills above it where the timber is needed to modify the storms of winter.

Very naturally timber cutters prefer to cut as near town as possible, and along the mountain roads, and above the town so as to haul the wood down hill, but it would pay our property owners much better to pay more for their wood and have it cut farther from town and where the falling of the trees will not destroy the value and appearance of Ouray property.

Is there no law applying to this? If there is let some one hunt it up. September 2, 1881

The law regarding the wholesale destruction of timber for other than legitimate purposes should be enforced in this camp. January 20, 1882

Strangers from other camps should bear in mind that anyone firing timber through negligence or otherwise will receive an introduction to the vigilance committee. There is no excuse for such devastation. June 29 1883

Lawyers seemed to have been a pet peeve of Day, not to mention many of his contemporaries. Every so often, he would let loose a blast at them over some issue.

An attorney is a very nice thing to have when legal advice is necessary. But copying ordinances at $62.50 each is rather an expensive luxury. April 1, 1880

Barnum has discovered in a backwood's Maine village a lawyer who has been known to shovel the snow off the sidewalk in front of his office. April 15, 1880

The Ouray bar, with possibly two or three exceptions, may be classed as common, best common, very common and dam-common, the latter brand predominating. September 30, 1881

The Ouray bar association after a series of meetings decided upon charging as follows; first a retainer; second, a remainder; third, a refresher; fourth, a finisher. The two-meals-a-day plank was tabled, and a motion to accept trade dollars, cord –wood and meal tickets at par was acted upon favorably. May 23, 1884

As stated previously, Day could not resist a few jabs at Colorado's most famous mining man, Horace Tabor, and his matrimonial problems. He divorced his first wife, Augusta, for the beautiful, but scandalous, divorcee Elizabeth Doe, or "Baby Doe" as she was better known. He secretly got a divorce in Durango, followed by a secret marriage in St. Louis, before officially divorcing Augusta in January of 1883, and remarrying Baby Doe in a glamorous wedding in Washington at the end of his thirty-day senatorial term.

Tabor's seat for thirty days in the U.S. Senate is said to have cost him $200,000.
A big price for so short a whistle.
Senator Tabor's forthcoming work entitled "Thirty days in the United States Senate," will be looked for with interest, as the crowning effort of his life. February 9, 1883

It is the wise buck, who anticipated the fawning season by providing himself with a Doe.—Horace A. W. March 9, 1883

Ex-senator Tabor, in addition to a seventy-five thousand dollar necklace, gave his bride a heart unspotted, and virtue without a blemish. Veracity, we'll see you later. March 9, 1883

Colorado is indebted to Tabor and Bill Byers [founder Rocky Mountain News] *for the only two real heart-rending scandals she has ever enjoyed. March 16, 1883*

A sweet-scented mess been stirred up by Bill Bush resign-ing the management of the Tabor [Grand] Opera House in Denver. Bill not only resigned, but, as Tabor alleges, stole $2,000 of the old man's wealth. Cause: Mrs. Bush refused to call on Mrs. McCourt-Doe-Tabor, etc. April 27, 1883

Tabor's wealth gave to the wife who breasted the storms of adversity a ruined and desolate house; to him, a tarnished name, the memory of confidence betrayed, the wreck of polit-ical ambition, and a venture in matrimony that is more sus-ceptible than constant. June 1, 1883

Well, if the records of La Plata County are any criterion upon which to have a financial conjecture, we should say that Horace A. W. WAS STRICTLY AND EXCLUSIVELY double standard. DO YOU sabe? December 14, 1883

Occasionally, Day would hit upon a topic, such as the Chinese "problem," his youth, leap year, books, "cannibal" Alfred Packer, babies, and snobbishness. Without reservation, he gave his readers his views, whether they liked them or not.

The Chinese must go. This country wants wash bills which it can read—paying them is a secondary consolation. March 12, 1880

From the new Chinese treaty, we learn that the Chinese gov-ernment is as anxious to keep the celestials as we are to have them stay. January 21, 1881

Several of our little folks were out coasting yesterday morn-ing and it took us back, in thought to the dim distant of the far distant past when we took our red sled and best girl and went sliding down the hill. What is there more enjoyable to a youngster than a good hill, a new sled and a jolly, rosy-cheeked girl. October 27, 1881

Leap year gives young ladies and widows a gentleman's privilege in mining love. Denver News [no date]
"A gentleman's privilege"—some gentlemen assert that everything is fair in love. Now, so far as we are individually concerned there is no objection to female company on our part, providing said females behaves properly. To spend an hour, talking over crop prospects; mining enterprises, art; literature etc, with a nice young lady or widow, it is heavenly. March 19, 1880

Books are universally conceded to be delightful companions, not only on account of the instruction they never intrude upon us at importune moments when we are not in the mood for their society. If we happen to disagree with them, they do not resent it, as others are apt to do; "one of them is praise or blame," and they are friendly in spite of neglect. They are always at our service, and moreover, in their company we may travel the wide world over . . . . February 6, 1880

Packer says that he has no fears, and that he will face death without a murmur, but, at the same time, thinks that common humanity demands he be executed in a village where the dance houses have not forced the ministers out. As a jumping-off place, Lake City is perfectly horrid. April 20, 1883

We had fully intended to have made personal mention of Ed Wright's baby last week, but inasmuch as it is a girl, we pass. Nothing short of an 18 karat boy baby can dead head the MULDOON. *January 2, 1880*

One of Ouray nice ladies can't understand why it is that we can't have a ball or party without having to associate with "dining room girls." It is a shame. A burnin' shame, for a nice lady who hasn't sense enough to boil potatoes or energy enough to wash before breakfast to be compelled to affiliate with an honest, hard working girl. Oh, it breaks us all up. May 19, 1882.

Editor Day had his pet peeves, one of which focused on patent medicine ads. On more than one occasion, he advised his readers and blasted the offending companies.

We announce for the 365th time, that there are no circumstances under which a patent medicine 'ad' can gain admission to the columns of the Solid Muldoon. *This is official, positive, emphatic and unalterable. September 21, 1883*

The patent medicine fiends and advertising agents are flooding the Muldoon *office with 'rare propositions.' They make excellent kindling. December, 1883*

There are not circumstances under which a patent medicine, piano, organ or any other Jim Crow 'ad' can gain admission to the columns of the Muldoon. *December 14. 1883*

Despite appearances, sometimes Dave Day had a sentimental vein in his heart. His eulogy to "Pood" shows him at his "best" as does his requiem for a mule.

It is with a sentiment of sorrowful regret, intensified by tenderest sympathies for the bereaved, that we announce the death of Ed LeCalare's purp. The little one was aged 3 months, 4 days, 1 hour and 61 minutes. It lived just long enough to twine around the brief span of its babyhood a world of hope and clinging affection.

> *Put away that rubber nipple,*
> *Sot that milk can on the shelf;*
> *For our darling little Pood,*
> *Has done and lost hisself.*

December 23, 1881

Last Tuesday night, a weary pilgrim, sick unto death, plodded along the streets insearch of charity. A comfortable place to rest the sore and feeble bones was all that was begged, but a deaf ear was turned to the supplications; Ouray rapt in the arms of Morpheus, left him at the mercy of a cold and silent night. Death, generous death, touched his tired heart, and ere the dawn of day on a pile of rubbish, lay the lifeless corps (sic) of a mule. September 5, 1884

CHAPTER 13

Humor

he *Solid Muldoon* and its editor/owner David Day became well known for humor—about a chuckle or two an issue. Sometimes the humor was simply funny, at other times it had a sharp point, sometimes a humorous observation was made about an event or individual, and, at times, there was humor with perchance a bit of wisdom mixed in. Not infrequently, Day's prose would make fun of an individual; and it is this last category that is perhaps the most difficult for today's readers to enjoy. They often have no idea who the target of the humorous barb might have been, or why the comment "tickled" the *Muldoon* reader.

A sampling of this humor appears in an earlier chapter where the individual in question is a recognizable person today. However, rather than destroy Day's more dated humor by trying to explain hilarious observations from the past, this one aspect of the funny side of the *Muldoon* has been left out.

Otherwise, in the quotes that follow, Dave Day takes a bow at his quotable best. These selections illustrate the type of quips that made him and his paper famous or, depending on the reaction, infamous. Without question, Day probably borrowed some; but most seem to be his original text. He did put a disclaimer in his columns occasionally—"Of course our readers understand that this column is mostly made up of sheer nonsense."

> *The whiskey that biteth like a serpent is probably of the serpentine, that is to say "crooked kind." September 19, 1879*

> *If an editor's wife ever wore diamonds it was because her husband stuck to paste. September 19, 1879*

An individual who called his first daughter Kate when his wife surprised him with another girl, promptly christened it Duplicate. September 19, 1879

Marriageable women are scarce in Arizona, and, in the opinion of most marriageable women, marriageable men are equally scarce. September 19, 1879

During the Caribou [Colorado] conflagration a woman carried a barrel of flour down stairs without bursting a hoop. In ordinary times it exhausts her to strike her husband twice with a poker. October 3, 1879

A physician has discovered yellow fever germs in ice. The safest way is to boil your ice before using it. This kills the germs. October 3, 1879

Never step on a dog's tail, unless the other end of the dog is a mile away from the tail. October 3, 1879

Eve was the heroine of the first and biggest snake story on record. October 3, 1879

If Edison really wishes to benefit the human race he will invent a faucet that will draw a glass of beer with the foam on the bottom. October 10, 1879

Always make it a rule to never say anything to a man's face that you wouldn't dare say behind his back. October 10, 1879

A Lake City mother chastised her daughter for winking at a lawyer. It wasn't the winking part that the old lady particularly objected to, but the idea of a girl of eighteen years old not being able to "atingush tween a siety nd trash." November 7, 1879

It don't require much of an effort on our part to raise the devil—he sleeps in the office. December 5, 1879

No true lady will bounce out of the room and slam the door after her when asked to forego her new dress for a few days and let her husband settle an old cigar bill. December 19, 1879

The way to fill a hall is to charge an admiration of fifty cents, then secretly distribute deadhead tickets. All who receive one will go. December 19, 1879

Great men pay high prices for choice library books, make a show of them, die, and their heirs sell out for what they will bring. December 19, 1879

The astronomer's business is looking up. January 9, 1880

The wind always finds something to blow about. January 9, 1880

Kisses by telephone taste like a boiled china egg on toast. January 9, 1880

There is much happiness in money. The only trouble is to get the amount right. January 9, 1880

A woman never grows old. As soon as she passes twenty-five she hides the family Bible. January 16, 1880

A match is light-headed when it comes to the scratch. January 30, 1880

A hen is a model for dancers. She never leaves her set except to eat and drink. January 30, 1880

There are too few men following the plow in this country and too many following the women. January 30, 1880

The farmer always finds mower work to do in the summer than in winter. January 30, 1880

Put up job—hoisting your umbrella. February 18, 1880

An exchange says many a plant is ruined by too much soaking. So is many a man. February 18, 1880

A good boy may not become a handsome man, but a nice bonnet surely becomes a pretty woman. February 18, 1880

College professor (to junior who has been taking advantage of his absent-mindedness) "young man," I find on looking over the records that this makes the fiftieth time in two years that you have been granted leave of absence to attend your grandmother's funeral. February 18, 1880

It only needs the climbing ivy to make some of Ouray's smelters picturesque ruins. April 16, 1880

It is easy enough to start a paper—keeping it going is what exercises the inventive genius. April 16, 1880

Poker-players epitaph—"Heaven called him." May 14, 1880

[Henry Ward] Beecher says heaven will never forgive a man of drowning a cat. Doesn't need to; nothing to forgive. May 14, 1880

What's the use of a college student kicking a foot-ball for five years only to graduate as a lawyer? May 14, 1880

The report that the baby elephant was born with a valise instead of a trunk is incorrect. May 14, 1880

The bowie knife has a fine rip-youtation. June 25, 1880

A college commencement is a queer thing, it begins at the end. June 25, 1880

'Early to bed, early to rise;' it was always so, in the season of flies. June 25, 1880

There would be more Artic expeditions if there were women at the poles. June 25, 1880

When you hear a rushing torrent of profanity it is a sign that a dam has burst. June 25, 1880

Love makes many a good right arm go to waist. June 25, 1880

"Tis love that makes the world go round." It also makes the young man go round—to the home of his girl about seven nights per week. June 25, 1880

The man who gets maddest at a newspaper squib is usually the fellow who borrows the paper he read it out of. June 25, 1880

The women over at Capitol [mining camp] ride on both sides of the saddle—but then a Capital woman would ri-do most anything. September 17, 1880

A debtor's tree—wil-lowe. November 26, 1880

If I wanted to conduct a paper in an intelligent community I would go back to the states. November 26, 1880

Blood relations—war stories. November 26 1880

A grate singer—the tea-kettle. November 26, 1880

A good fish country—fin-land. November 26, 1880

The man who thinks "the world owes him a living," will probably find it in the almshouse. November 26, 1880

Knowledge is better than wealth, yet how many people are there in this wicked world that prefer the inferior article. November 26, 1880

A man's best friends are his ten fingers. December 24, 1881

Society says one thing, and nature says another. December 24, 1881

Any kind of an honest job is better than no job at all. December 24, 1881

False issues—counterfeit bank bills. December 31, 1880

The board of education—the black board. December 31, 1880

Bakers are the most persistent loafers in the world. February 4, 1881

All the world's a stage—and very few good players.
February 4, 1881

At this point, Day apparently felt more confident to aim his jokes at local people and Colorado in general. Consequently, his humor shifted, as will be seen in the following examples. The variety is also better and more biting in some respects. Unfortunately many of his humorous shots go unappreciated today because, as mentioned, the targets fail to be familiar.

> *The maid who adorns the knee of her lover while the gas is turned down is "borne to blush unseen." February 4, 1881*

> *One of Ouray's young ladies has been practicing preparatory to organizing an archery club. The firers attempt to paralyze a twenty-foot target disgusted the cat. June 3, 1881*

> *Pueblo had a "social event," but the Chieftain didn't say whether it was a boy or a girl. December 2, 1881*

> *When a Ourayite skips the town a few hundred short, his friends give out that he has "readjusted." December 2, 1881*

> *Pueblo is threatened with a coal famine. Nothing short of a whiskey famine will ever completely unsettle this people. December 9, 1881*

> *The beautiful weather took a slight cold Thursday but is itself again. February 17, 1882*

> *An item is going the rounds of eastern press headed "A virtuous virgin." Wonder who it can mean? February 17, 1882*

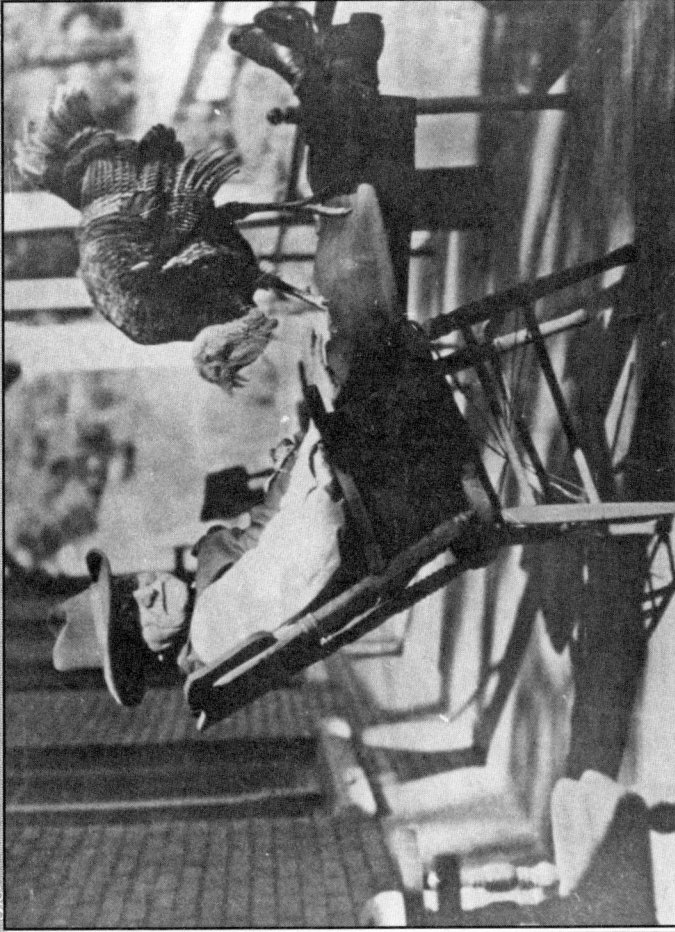

Dave Day had no trouble poking fun at people, including himself. Western Historical Collection, University of Colorado

Look out for picnic. It is about the season of the year when they sprout. March 31, 1882

Eugene Field [the poet was, at this time, editor of the *Denver Tribune*] *rescued from a "watery grave" on Sunday last. Mr. Field, we fear, has contacted some very reckless habits since leaving Missouri. Little did we think that one who was reared among its secret stills that dot the isolated glens along the beautiful Kaw would ever so far forget his early teaching as to disrobe and rush frantically into a whole puddle of real water. "Gene water you thinking about." June 23, 1882*

The wagon road between Ouray and the Park is sadly in need of repairs. Entirely too many rocks for the amount of toll collected. August 4, 1882

Owing to the two bears being rounded up this week, mothers will have something to frighten disobedient children with by telling them if they are naughty the bears will come down out of the mountains and eat them up, and the kids will respond: "Go up old bald head, go up." [quote from *McGuffey Electric Readers,* the most popular school books in Day's youth] *August 4, 1882*

Girls who reside back east and do all the washing and kitchen work for less than two dollars per week, can, by washing alone, command two dollars per day in Ouray and if so disposed, get in seven days per week. There is no Sunday in this country worth speaking of—the altitude you know. March 2, 1883

The United States streamer Ashuelot is lost in Chinese waters. This thing of allowing vessels belonging to the American navy to get out of sight of dry land is expensive and uncalled for. March 2, 1883

Hell hath no nuisance like unto a female gossip. March 2, 1883

Never run into debt, not if you can find anything else to run into. April 27, 1883

Marry young; if you make a hit keep cool and don't brag about it. April 27, 1883

Exercise in open air, but don't saw wood until you are obliged to. April 27, 1883

Job, who during his lifetime acquired some reputation for patience, was never subjected to the blighting task of listening to a country lawyer on Decoration Day. June 1, 1883

A young lady of twenty-two autumns asks what is the proper thing to do when she is serenaded at a late hour by a gentleman. Well, sissy, untie the dog and turn loose a basin of slop. No sensible man ever prospects with a brass band. October 19, 1883

The discovery of the body of a dead rabbit in the reservoir is a powerful argument against prohibition in mountain towns. March 7, 1884

Nothing calls to mind the delights and comforts of a single blessedness so vividly as to find your wife has been sloshing around in your slippers and stretched them all-our of shape, or discovery 'little tootsy-wootsy' has been eating crackers in bed. March 7, 1884

When an Ouray woman grows tired of this life she don't load her stomach with deadly drugs and terrify the entire neighborhood. She just marries a lawyer and allows starvation to do the shuffling. Something philosophical about those Ouray, so there is. March 14. 1882

Millions have been expended in attempting to reach the North Pole, and yet we know as little of that far off land as the average Denver Republican editor does of the Five-cent Fare bill. Absolutely nothing. July 25, 1884

The nights are growing sufficiently chilly to suggest two in a bed spoon fashion. August 29, 1884

Red hair is quite fashionable, and it is even reported that artificial means are resorted to in order to procure the desirable shade which is a happy cross between a ratification meeting and a Kansas sunset. December 5, 1889

The Uncompahgre River is so low that the suckers are employed to pull the trout over the riffles, and the mallard ducks so disgusted with the outlook that they have flown Utahwards in search of more prohibition. December 5, 1889

Among Ouray's citizens are two ex-confederate and two ex-federal colonels, one ex-congressman, one ex-U.S. Judge and ex-majors, captains and lieutenants without end. December 5, 1889

About all the private boardinghouses in Ouray have suspended, but the average private boarder eats more and pays less than even a lawyer. December 5, 1884

There must be pay rock in sight when you can get your girl a diamond ring. January 23, 1885

Every lady who is a subscriber to Harper's Bazaar *wonders how it is that her sex can get along without that most excellent publication. We are inclined to believe that no well regulated family can dispense with it. January 23, 1885*

EPILOGUE
-30-

What may be written as an epilogue to this tale of Editor David F. Day, Ouray, and his *Solid Muldoon*? Whether one agreed with him or not, he certainly helped make Ouray better known. His quips, comments and articles were often quoted in other newspapers. People throughout the West, and probably beyond, gained some inkling of Ouray as involved, funny, a cross section of America, or intriguing. They might sometimes wonder about the editor, but usually chuckled with him, unless he hit too close to home.

An ardent supporter of mining, particularly at Red Mountain and those districts near Ouray, Day proved to be a "booster" and a "watchdog." He called down fraudulent mining companies, schemes, and owners who picked investors' pocketbooks rather than invest the funds in actual mining. Failures and sudden closures caught his attention as well. All of these would give Ouray a bad name, something that Dave Day would not tolerate.

In his own way, he worked to promote a better community and quality of life for its residents. For example, he supported schools and cleaning the streets but opposed the red-light district, when it overstepped its bounds. He must have driven some "city fathers" to the brink. Beware, however, those who spent taxpayer money frivolously or incompetently on projects the editor did not approve of for whatever reason or reasons. Day's sharp pen could burst a balloon quicker than it could be sent a-rising. His "damn the torpedoes" approach pleased not everyone, but, as mentioned several times, that failed to bother him.

There can be no question that the *Muldoon*, in its own inimitable way, helped make Ouray a better community. Day prodded, poked, and agitated, making the council members and locals aware of some need or problem. He would not let up until it was done.

Politically, he was a thorn in the side of Republicans, a gadfly who never retreated. The Democratic Party could count on his support, although sometimes with less than enthusiasm. Individual candidates would be wise not to stir the editor too much for fear of some unwanted publicity.

Personally fearless, Dave Day would launch campaigns about a variety of issues. He could be threatened but not coerced. This Medal of Honor recipient had been through Shiloh, Vicksburg, a host of skirmishes, and Confederate prisoner of war camps, so fear and intimidation did not bother him.

Nor was he averse to "calling down" one of his journalistic colleagues, whether locally, statewide, or beyond. He would attack or defend with the best and still forge ahead. This trait called forth some of his best quips and articles, quite often to the embarrassment and disgust of his targeted contemporary or subject. Nor did libel suits seem to faze him in his youth, or even later in his career.

His writing (one might dare call it his literary style) was readable and memorable. He mastered the quick quip, the cutting remark, the unforgettable description, the pointed humor, the stalwart advice (or so he believed), and, last, but not least, sharp, clear, and focused writing. Not against being critical, Day would lambaste those who were sloppy in their writing and reporting.

David Frakes Day left another mark on history. He engaged and enlightened his era for the present and the future. Perhaps that was his greatest contribution, the ability to make people and places come alive for readers of his day and later. For those who would take the time to read, Day preserved the life and times of a community, its people, and its hopes, dreams, and perhaps its nightmares.

Henry James, writing the then famous educator, editor, and fellow writer, Charles Eliot Norton, in January 1871, observed:

The face of nature and civilization in this our country is to a certain point a very sufficient literary field. But it will yield its secrets only to a really grasping imagination. . . . To write well and worthily of American things one need even more than elsewhere to be a master.

In his own way and style, Day strived to reach that goal.

To return one more time to Mark Twain and his observations. Among his comments on writing are several that could serve as an epitaph for David Day.

The difference between the right word and the almost right word is the difference between lightning and the lightning bug.

The author shall say what he is proposing to say, not merely come near it.

My books are water; those of the great geniuses is wine. Everybody drinks water.

Indeed, Day wrote for everybody, clearly and forcefully. He could ask for no greater legacy.

INDEX